IN SEARCH OF FATHERHOOD®—

TRANSCENDING BOUNDARIES

IN SEARCH OF FATHERHOOD®—

Transcending Boundaries

Diane A. Sears

To order additional copies of this book, contact:
Xlibris Corporation
1-888-795-4274
www.Xlibris.com
Orders@Xlibris.com
22586

CONTENTS

ACKNOWLEDGEMENTS

To My Family: I am buoyed by and thankful for your individual and collective sacrifices and unconditional love.

To My Mentor—L.T. Henry: The resurrection of your vision illuminates the darkness created by your passing.

To The Fathers of the World: Thank you for mentoring, nurturing and loving our children.

I am eternally grateful to Stephen Baskerville, Ph.D., Warren Farrell, Ph.D., Thomas Golden, LCSW, Alvin F. Poussaint, M.D. and Messrs. Muhammad Nasser Bey, Randy L. Collins, Leonard Dantzler, Dale Fraza, Thomas Hoerner, Gary A. Johnson, James Kennedy, Thomas Lessman, Martin G. Ramey, Almas Jamil Sami', and Joep Zander for their invaluable contributions to this book project. I have learned so much from each of you.

I am equally grateful to Fathers' Rights activists and Fatherhood organizations in the United States, Europe, Australia and New Zealand for their invaluable support during the past four years.

INTRODUCTION

In many ways—and for many reasons—Fatherhood transcends the boundaries of geography, ethnicity, religion, language, culture, politics and economics. Men who are Fathers from all Walks of Life throughout our global village experience the joys and challenges of raising children as they discover that a magic formula for parenting does not exist. Collectively and unceremoniously—and in some instances, under the most difficult set of circumstances—Single Fathers, Married Fathers, Divorced Fathers, "Stay-At-Home" Fathers, "Long-Distance" Fathers, Custodial Fathers and Non-Custodial Fathers from all Walks of Life throughout our global village shape the minds and souls of their children. They worry about the world that their children will inherit when they reach adulthood. Their children's health and physical safety are of primary concern. Men wonder if they are being good parents as they struggle to develop and implement plans that will move their families forward. No one has come to them and said, "To become a successful parent and have happy, well-adjusted children, you need to do 'x, y and z'." Each new day presents Men who are Fathers with a unique set of questions and issues directly and indirectly related to Fatherhood. All Men who are Fathers are searching for answers to questions about Fatherhood. Men who are Fathers find themselves grappling with an incessant flow of issues. This universal search for answers and quest to resolve issues has provided Men who are Fathers with an opportunity to closely scrutinize their roles and responsibilities as parents.

IN SEARCH OF FATHERHOOD®—TRANSCENDING BOUNDARIES candidly explores the daunting questions and issues that confront Single Fathers, Married Fathers, "Stay-At-Home" Fathers, Divorced Fathers, "Long-Distance" Fathers, Custodial

Fathers and Non-Custodial Fathers. The gentlemen that you will meet on the pages that follow—*Stephen Baskerville, Ph.D., Muhammad Nasser Bey, Randy L. Collins, Leonard Dantzler, Warren Farrell, Ph.D., Dale Fraza, Thomas Golden, LCSW, the late L.T. Henry, Thomas Hoerner, Gary A. Johnson, James Kennedy, Thomas Lessman, Alvin F. Poussaint, M.D., Martin G. Ramey, Almas Jamil Sami' and Joep Zander*—speak profoundly about the roles and responsibilities of Men who are Fathers and the joys and challenges of Fatherhood. **IN SEARCH OF FATHERHOOD®**—TRANSCENDING BOUNDARIES examines how Men who are Fathers from all Walks of Life influence their children's perception of the world outside of their environment and offers suggestions about what our young men need from us as they make the journey from childhood to manhood.

IN SEARCH OF FATHERHOOD®—TRANSCENDING BOUNDARIES is a reaffirmation of Fatherhood. **IN SEARCH OF FATHERHOOD®**—TRANSCENDING BOUNDARIES is also a reaffirmation of the vision of a Forum for Fathers which was conceived by my late mentor—L.T. Henry—a classically trained jazz musician, author, photojournalist and sales and motivation trainer. Unfortunately, he died before he could develop his idea. It was his belief that Men who are Fathers from all Walks of Life throughout our global village had unanswered questions about Fatherhood and that they were engaged in a silent and never-ending search for answers. His vision, through **IN SEARCH OF FATHERHOOD®**—TRANSCENDING BOUNDARIES, has been transformed into something that everyone can see, feel, hear and touch. It was the least that I could do for a Man who had done so much for me.

STEPHEN BASKERVILLE, PH.D.

FATHERS' RIGHTS ARE FATHERS' DUTIES

Separation and divorce destroy children's lives. It helps to remember this because of the vast industry now devoted to what has been called "good divorce." This is the trend that seems intent on making divorce palatable and letting parents feel good about destroying their children's home. At best this is damage control. It is impossible to insulate children from the damage caused by the destruction of their families. Those who pretend we can are lying to themselves and to us. Moreover, the traumas of divorce are almost all exacerbated by litigation. Worse, they are all exacerbated when one parent—usually the father—is marginalized from the children, as is now almost invariably the case.

The reasons why separation and divorce damage children are too numerous to mention. But from the standpoint of fatherhood politics, the most important reasons involve authority.

The very act of separation and divorce, aside from any accompanying behavior or words, itself sends a myriad of terrible messages to children. It says that parents can put their own wishes above the welfare of their children. This is obviously a bad example, which the children can then carry on to their own families. But, perhaps, a worse effect is to destroy parental authority. No parent who has put himself or herself before their child in such a basic way has any moral authority to instruct, correct, or discipline a child. How can parents instill lessons of selflessness in children when their own actions demonstrate precisely the opposite?

More specifically, it destroys notions of trust, obligation, and fidelity in the child, qualities basic to any family. In effect it says that it is okay to break promises and obligations such as marriage vows when they no longer suit our convenience, it is okay to make up the rules as we go along and, in effect, live by no principles except those that suit our momentary convenience. Again, how can parents instill an ethic of fidelity, obligation, and trust when their own actions manifest the contrary?

Even more fundamentally, it destroys the integrity of the family itself. The act of separation and divorce says that a family is not something from which the child can derive a sense of unconditional love and security. On the contrary, a family can be disbanded at any time at the whim of one member. Even more, it says that a family member can be disgraced and expelled. Especially when it is unilateral (as it increasingly is) and when one parent is marginalized from the children's lives, the effect is the expulsion of a family member. This is the destruction of the child's entire world and the source of unimaginable terror to a child. If Daddy can be pushed out of the family, after all, what about me? What security is there in my family if members can be expelled because they do something Mommy or someone else doesn't like? What if I do something Mommy doesn't like? What is the meaning of Mommy's or Daddy's love if it can be terminated when it is no longer convenient?

Finally, litigation against family members exacerbates and in effect politicizes these messages. It says that the state is a legitimate instrument to punish the child's loved one who has fallen out of favor. It says that rather than solving problems as a family, we declare a member to be a public enemy and bring the power of the state to bear on him. In an almost literal sense, we declare civil war on our loved ones. Again, if the police can be used to keep Daddy away or throw him in jail because Mommy no longer likes him, what will they do to me?

Perhaps from the political standpoint, the most significant lesson for the child is the firsthand experience of tyranny and oppression, both in society and within his own family. The custodial parent becomes a kind of satrap of the court, and the dictatorship of the court over the family is extended and writ small within the family. The custodial parent tyrannizes over the non-custodial parent, undermining his authority, dictating the terms of his access to the children, talking to him contemptuously and condescendingly as if he were himself a naughty child, perhaps engaging in a full scale campaign of vilification (which similarly mirrors the larger campaign against fathers waged by the state and media). After witnessing this against the non-custodial parent, the children then experience it themselves. With no checks on the power of the custodial parent, the tyranny is naturally exercised over them as well. In extreme (but not uncommon) cases, of course, this leads to child abuse.

All these messages concern authority—parental authority, paternal authority, political authority—and therefore they are of primary interest to fathers.

When a father participates in separation and divorce, when he engages in litigation, when he even acquiesces in them, he too, is sending these messages to his children. When a father takes part in these actions he is participating in the destruction of his own authority. He is taking part in the destruction of his own fatherhood.

Certainly there are times when we must resort to the courts just to be permitted to see our children. But in the long run when we rely on these means, when we allow them to dictate the terms and place of the struggle, we lose and so do our children. Even when these actions are undertaken by our spouses unilaterally, the child is receiving the same message. Then it is up to us alone to provide a positive counter-message.

The literature on "good divorce" offers no rebuttals to these messages. There is a more effective and more constructive alternative.

The Political Alternative

The alternative is to become active politically for the defense of our children and families.

I know this idea immediately raises red flags among many. Images come to mind of strident "activists" (like the dreaded feminists perhaps) screeching about their "rights." Many men are uncomfortable in this role, in which they have never before seen themselves. Our political world has become such a plethora of competing interest groups all trying to grab their share of the pie that we have forgotten what political action has done to relieve the truly oppressed.

More serious is the common assumption among men that working politically for the rights of fathers and children will divert time and energy from their own individual legal cases and reduce time with their own children while resulting in few tangible benefits in terms of winning custody or increasing visitation. This is a natural assumption, but it is not true.

In fact, the opposite is true. Political involvement may be the best thing you can do for your own case and for your own children. Moreover, it will be beneficial to you and your children immediately, even if you never achieve the stated goals. It is more effective than all the touchy-feely advice you will get from therapists. And it is more constructive than all the legal help from the scavengers of the divorce industry. This is less because of what it gives than what it demands: It requires qualities that are directly necessary to fathers who have been through desertion, separation, divorce, false accusations, and the rest. Most importantly, it carries messages that can help heal the traumas of children who are suffering from separation and divorce.

Here are some of the direct and immediate benefits of political action:

Political action establishes authority. If you have gone through a desertion, separation, or divorce—especially if your child was abducted from your home or you have been accused of some kind of abuse—your authority as a father has been largely destroyed. Even fathers in intact families have felt their authority take quite a drubbing these days, largely owing to the anti-male climate. If your wife has placed her desires before her children's welfare by destroying their home, she too, no longer has any moral authority to correct a child. Political action gives you the authority of one who has taken the moral high ground and acts out of principle along with others through constructive means for the welfare and establishment of his family and his society.

Political action confers dignity. When you lost your children you lost your dignity and received the stigma of the "evil male." You unexpectedly joined the ranks of "abusers," "batterers," and "deadbeat dads." Suddenly all those things you assumed about others are being assumed about you. You "must have" done something to deserve losing your children. This is a very difficult stigma to remove, and you won't eliminate it by cowering behind a lawyer. Men do not hire someone else to fight their battles. Standing up for your rights and those of your children is a way of proclaiming to the world that you have nothing to be ashamed of and that you have done nothing wrong.

Properly understood, political action is not shrill or strident. It is the dignified but uncompromising demand for civil rights: the right to be fathers to your children. No political movement ever has lasting success without dignity, and fathers will get nowhere unless they show dignity both in their families and before the world. No doubt you have already discovered that in the home it is up to you to act maturely and not to quarrel with your spouse, because of the bias in the courts and because your spouse probably has no incentive to be restrained. Why not take this one step further into the public realm and forego the quarrel of a court battle? The same principle applies. We don't have to hide our actions from our children or anyone else because they are ugly, undignified, shameful, or vicious—as is, for example, beating up on our spouse in a courtroom with a hired goon. We are acting openly in the public realm. We are asking for justice in the court of public opinion. Nothing could be more dignified.

Political action will make you a better father. The qualities necessary for being an effective political activist are the same as those necessary for a good father: sobriety, commitment, fidelity, sacrifice. Demanding your just rights is not a license for belligerence; quite the opposite. All great revolutionary leaders were moral puritans who saw the need for self-discipline. Lenin used to inveigh against libertine communists who would substitute talk for action and initiate a dozen tasks and never complete any. If you don't like this comparison, consider Oliver Cromwell, who "conquered himself" before he conquered his enemies. Frederick Douglass gave up drinking because he saw it was the most effective method of slaveholders to keep his people in bondage. Martin Luther King used to speak of the need for "self-purification" prior to action. The principle is simple: self-government requires self-control. Alcohol, gambling, womanizing, frivolous pastimes are incompatible with republican virtue. If you can't give up your sports page or your evenings in front of the TV, your girlie magazines or your nights out with the lads, you're no use as a fathers' rights activist. You're also probably not the world's greatest father.

Political action is an effective alternative to violence. Without lending credence to the hysteria over "male violence," let us grant for the sake of argument that fathers may be tempted to become violent when their children are taken away (who wouldn't?). If you find disturbing thoughts suddenly appearing in your head when they take your children, channel it into peaceful and constructive but determined activity for your children. Martin Luther King used to observe that violence in the black ghettoes decreased significantly following political demonstrations. Involvement in fathers' rights is an effective way of channeling rage that might otherwise fuel domestic violence.

Political action shows your child you care. You may be caught in the vicious circle of being ordered to stay away from your children by a judge and as a result having them think you don't love them because you're not there. This is their natural conclusion and could be exacerbated by Mom's poison. You can't tell them it's because of Mommy or the Evil Judge that you aren't there, and you shouldn't; even if you could it wouldn't matter. Children judge by actions, not words. On the other hand, once your children witness you exercising your civic duty and your constitutional rights on their behalf and on behalf of other fathers and children, they will eventually understand why. They will realize that political action requires sacrifice, and they will admire you all the more and profit from your example. You are also telling the world that your children are so special that their father is willing to sacrifice everything for them.

Political action is an excellent education for your children. Some fathers feel they must not involve their children in their quarrel and fear they may be punished for it. But this is true only because the conflict is personal and litigious; in other words, because it is shameful. Children should always be spared the trauma of quarreling parents and animosity between spouses, whether at home or in court. But exercising your civic rights—indeed, fulfilling your duty as a citizen—is a different matter entirely. This is something your children should see. We make enormous efforts in schools, churches, and civic organizations, teaching children about civic involvement, about constitutional rights and the importance of cultivating a public spirit and of sacrificing private desires for the larger public good. We introduce them to the teachings of Socrates, Thoreau, Gandhi, and Martin Luther King. Yet when it comes to putting their ideas into practice by following their example, we are told this is somehow "inappropriate." In contrast to litigation, when we undertake political action we are not fighting our children's mothers; we are fighting injustice. What could be more inspiring than to emulate these men on behalf of your children? Children know that actions speak louder than words. The lesson that civic action requires sacrifice, and must be undertaken with dignity, is both edifying for them and something that will make them proud of their father.

Finally, political action will provide your children with the spiritual tools they need to cope with family breakdown. This may not be obvious, yet it is true. But only if it is based on dignity, sacrifice, and love. A politics of hate, vengeance, and demonization is not a fit lesson for children. But a politics of love and non-violence has its origins in the same spiritual values we try to instill in our children in school and in church. No child is too young to learn this lesson. If you take your children to Sunday school (and many people feel this is an important duty of a father, even if he himself has previously not been religious), you will be exposing them to the courageous acts of the Hebrew women, of Shedrach,

Meshach, and Abednego, of Jesus himself. These figures demonstrated precisely the qualities children of divorce more than others need to see. Teach them about sacrifice for others, about commitment to a cause, about obligation as citizens, about the power of moral authority, about love to those who hate us, about fidelity to principles larger than themselves.

Martin Luther King, the leading American practitioner of nonviolence, used to talk about the latent violence in the system of state-enforced segregation and of the need for a "creative tension" to bring this violence out into the open. We have a similar task. A latent violence already pervades our families which are in effect occupied by the instruments of the state forcibly separating us from our children. We must extract the violence from the system, and we must be prepared to suffer violence ourselves, but we must use none. At some point we may have to adopt Ghandi's principle: "Fill up the jails."

No doubt you will be accused of dragging your children into the quarrel. But non-violent political action shifts the quarrel away from the person to the injustice. Our children are already at the center of the quarrel. They have already been dragged in as the chief victims by the belligerent parent and by the state that has invaded their family and set up a kind of domestic apartheid between the custodial parent and the child, on the one hand, and the non-custodial parent. Martin Luther King writes boldly and eloquently of how, despite the false pathos of those who "deplored our 'using' our children in this fashion . . . the introduction of Birmingham's children into the [non-violent civil rights] campaign was one of the wisest moves we made."

It is an illusion to pretend that we can shelter our children from a quarrel of which they are at the center and which by its very nature is constantly damaging them. What is important is not that they be sheltered from it but that they be provided with the tools to deal with it and with any crisis constructively. On their own what they will adopt are the tools of withdrawal, guilt, aggression, alienation, or any number of other symptoms of divorce that have become all too familiar. No matter how careful you are they will also absorb your hostility as well as that of your spouse.

The touchy-feely proponents of "good divorce" are right as far as they go when they tell us how to mitigate these emotions and suggest we "talk" to our children to mitigate these emotions. They suggest you tell your children, "No matter what we do to one another, your Mommy and I still love you." But consciously or not, the child knows, "but not enough to keep my home together." You are supposed to tell your child, "What's happening between Mommy and me is not your fault." But the child knows that he or she is the center and "cause" of the quarrel. Talk is cheap, and children know it. No amount of talk, contact group jargon, or therapy sessions is going to save children from the traumas of what their parents do. What we can do is give them the tools to overcome them and to act. These are partly spiritual, but they are also political.

The Bible and the Koran teach that we are all guilty of sin. Creative non-violence teaches that we are all responsible for society's injustices. Choose the value system you prefer. The point is that these religious and political values teach us how we and our children can channel our inadequacies, real and imagined, into constructive action.

We should tell our children that we all do bad things. We are all sinners, or we are all responsible for society's injustices, or however you prefer to phrase it. We cannot avoid guilt. What we can do is be sorry for the bad things we do and ask forgiveness. What we can do is forgive those who do bad things to us. What we can do is to love the person while hating the evil they do—the message of Christianity, Islam, civil disobedience, creative non-violence, and every other humane doctrine. We can teach them what the Bible, Gandhi, and Martin Luther King all taught that "unmerited suffering is redemptive." We can teach them the one central principle of both religion and political action: that salvation requires sacrifice. If we strive toward this, we will not only have happy, well-adjusted children in spite of the belligerence they witness in others; we may just be permitted to be fathers to them again. Or perhaps I should say, that from that moment, we again will be fathers.

THE POLITICS OF FATHERHOOD

When we first conceived the idea for a conference on "The Politics of Fatherhood" not everyone was sure precisely what it would mean. And perhaps we were not sure ourselves. We knew the fatherhood crisis had been addressed by several disciplines and that political science was not one of them. As a student of political thought, I knew that most major political theorists have had something to say about the place of fatherhood in civil society and the role of father as preparative for that of citizen. We also knew that any social movement inevitably involves politics, both internally among the various strands and externally in connection to the wider society and the public state.

We knew as well that one very politically-charged issue was central to this, as to every problem of American society—if I may be the one to be so direct—*race*. While the Fatherhood crisis has long been felt most acutely in minority communities, it can no longer be dismissed by the majority. As Cornel West and Sylvia Ann Hewlitt wrote in *The War On Parents*, "When it comes to . . . dads, the African-American experience prefigures the contemporary mainstream experience—and the results are devastating."

Indeed, given the gravity of the Fatherhood crisis, perhaps what we are seeing here is an unexpected validation of the prophecy of Frederick Douglass, who said that "the Negro and the nation are to rise or fall, be . . . saved or lost, together."

If this prophecy is indeed still valid, it means that the stakes are high for all of us. It means that in addressing the destruction of Fatherhood in the minority community, we are simultaneously addressing it for the majority and throughout our society.

It may also mean that the experiences of the minority in recent decades are applicable here. Among the lessons of the civil rights movement that might be profitable for those of us to see our task as creating empowerment for fathers is that no people can be empowered by others; by definition, the only way to be empowered is to empower oneself. And power means politics.

This has not been the central approach thus far in the Fatherhood movement. Yet sooner or later, it is one we must confront. If for no other reason than the rather startling fact that, with the exception of convicted criminals, no group in our society today has fewer rights than Fathers,—not unwed fathers, not divorced fathers. Even accused criminals have the right to due process, to know the charges against them, to a lawyer, and to a trial. A father can be deprived of his children, his home and life savings, and his freedom with none of these constitutional protections. It will come as no surprise to some here that the line between fathers and criminals is now becoming thin. This is sometimes owing to what fathers themselves have done. More often, it is the result of what our social, political, and legal system has done.

Nowhere is the criminalization of Fatherhood more evident than in the politics of the judiciary. It is the courts which, from the days of the civil rights movement, we have looked to as the guardians of the constitutional rights of individuals and minorities. Yet for fathers and families generally, the judiciary has not only failed to protect constitutional rights; it has become their principal violator.

The arm of the state that undeniably reaches deepest into the private lives of individuals and families today is the family court. Malcolm X once described a family court as modern "slavery," and more recently, West and Hewlitt have written that "the entire process seems to bypass most constitutional protections." The very notion of a "family court"—now backed up by a vast array of family police—should alert us to danger.

Yet far from scrutinizing these bodies, we give them virtually unchecked power. Shrouded in secrecy and leaving no record of their proceedings, they are accountable to virtually no one. Robert W. Page, Presiding Judge of the Family Part of the Superior Court of New Jersey, writes that "the power of family court judges is almost unlimited."

Predictably, with unlimited power, the family courts of this country are now out of control. They are not tribunals for redressing injustice; they are more of a racket for plundering fathers and funneling money into the pocket of lawyers. Though their lips are dripping with the words "best interest of the child," they are in fact using our children as weapons and as commodities for the increase of their own power and profit.

We have in our history seen the consequences of treating an entire class of citizens as if the Bill of Rights did not apply to them. We have tried to live in a "house divided"—in a political system that operates "half slave" and "half free." And we have found, as Lincoln warned, that sooner or later it must be all one or all the other.

As a society, we are always in danger of forgetting what we have learned, and I think it is the appropriate role of this University, with its role in the history of civil rights, to remind us. For it is the responsibility of scholars, perhaps more than others, to point out and criticize the abuse of power. "The neutral scholar is an ignoble man," wrote Frederick Douglass. "The future public opinion of the land . . . must redound to the honor of the scholars . . . or cover them with shame."

What we are now seeing, to paraphrase Douglass, is the authoritarian power of the courts advancing, "poisoning, corrupting, and perverting the institutions of the country." In fact, what we are witnessing today may be the most massive institutionalized witch hunt in this country's history.

Never before have we seen, on such scale, mass incarcerations without trial, without charge, and without counsel—while the media and civil libertarians look the other way.

Never before have we seen the spectacle of the highest officials in our land—including the President of the United States, the Attorney General and major cabinet secretaries, and leading members of Congress from both parties—using their office as a platform to publicly vilify private citizens who have been convicted of nothing and who have no opportunity to reply.

Never before have we seen government officials walk so freely into the homes of private citizens who are accused of nothing and help themselves to whatever they want, including their children, their life savings, their private papers and effects, and eventually, their persons.

Not since the days of Communist Eastern Europe and Nazi Germany have we seen the regular use of children as informers against their parents.

Never before have we seen the stealing of children systematized to a bureaucratic routine. To find the forced separation of children from their parents on such a scale we must go back before the days of Communism and Nazism. Though both these regions routinely took children from their parents, they did so on a scale that was miniscule compared to what is now practiced in the United States. Indeed, we must return to the days of American slavery to find a time when state power was used to forcibly break up families on a scale comparable to what is taking place today.

It is not lightly that I invoke the slave system. It is to illustrate our experience that any system of domestic dictatorship—no matter how apparently "private" and apolitical—poses a serious threat to a democratic society. Nowhere is this more destructively seen than in the impact on our children themselves.

Politically, the decisive argument against slavery was not so much its physical cruelty as the corruption it wrought in the political system and in the minds and souls of what should have been free citizens. It fostered tyranny in the slaveholder, servility in the slaves, and moral degradation in both. Such habits of mind were said to be incompatible with the kind of republican virtue required for a free society.

The abolitionist Charles Sumner warned of the impact on the development of white children growing up in a slave society. "Their hearts, while yet tender with childhood, are necessarily hardened by this conduct, and their subsequent lives bear enduring testimony to this legalized uncharitableness," he wrote. "Their characters are debased, and they become less fit for the magnanimous duties of a good citizen."

Something similar is at work with the children who are now growing up under a state that forcibly destroys their families and their fathers. No people can remain free who harbor within themselves a system of dictatorship or raise their children according to its principles.

This too is "the politics of fatherhood."

MUHAMMAD NASSER BEY

"... THE TRUE JOY IS THE PRESENCE OF
MY SON AND MY WIFE IN MY LIFE ..."

He is a husband, a father, and a journalist in the print and electronic media. He holds down a full-time job; attends classes two evenings during each week where he is completing course work that will result in his becoming a network engineer and an information technology professional; and works to transform his dream of becoming a voiceover actor into reality. He is MUHAMMAD NASSER BEY.

How is Mr. Bey able to keep it all together? How is he able to play a dominant role in his child's life?

"First, let me say that the true joy is the presence of my son and wife in my life. Without them, my ambitions for school and work would not matter. This singular truth is the key to my sanity and without them, the rest does not matter," explains Mr. Bey. "To keep things together, I have a personal vision of myself—a positive vision that says there is nothing I cannot do. The secret to my success at keeping it all together is knowing that things change and that I have to move left and right when they do change in order to stay on course. Through a combination of hard work, patience, prayer and meditation on my goals, I am able to remain sane—remain honest with myself—and remain flexible."

And what, in Mr. Bey's views, are the joys of Fatherhood?

"Ah, the joys of Fatherhood. The primary joy is knowing that, as of now, my son has beaten all the odds as have I. America long ago wrote the children of African descent off. My son by age 18 was supposed to have come from a broken home, lived without a strong male figure to emulate, done poorly in school, have a police record and have died in the inevitable drive-by or been strung out on drugs—but because of the efforts and love of his parents and grandparents none of these things have happened. My son is a junior in high school and attends college on the weekends."

So, what are the challenging aspects of Fatherhood?

"By far the greatest challenge is fighting the temptation to control or to try to control my son and to remember that he is an individual and not my property. For many men, love is conditional, especially where our sons are concerned. We show them favor if they do as we say. Most fathers want to guide, to push, and yes, to judge their sons, or worse to make them like themselves. But we cannot and should not try to. It is a mighty struggle indeed to fight the impulses to demand and offer examples, you know . . . 'when I was your age' . . . that sort of thing.

Children hear nothing you say, but see everything you do. The challenge here is in part not to do something to him that I did not want my father to do to me—to complement and share in his life and dreams without interfering in them. There is a real Freudian thing going on where this is concerned. I could go on about it, but I'll wait until the next interview."

I asked Mr. Bey if he was given any advice about Fatherhood. Who gave him the advice? And what was he told?

"No. No one ever sat me down and said 'This is what you do to be a good father.' Although there was advice here and there about life and living. Again, the example of others came into play for me. My own father came to school during parent-teacher meetings, showed up at my classroom door unexpected more than once—as recently as my days in 10th grade—checked homework, disciplined his sons, often with a heavy, but loving hand and apologized when he was wrong. I have tried to do the same. It seems to have worked. My son is quiet, strong and works hard in school. Indirectly, I was told by my parents' example to work hard, be honest, stay in school and stay out of trouble. That's all the advice that a Black kid growing up in the sixties and seventies needed."

When I asked Mr. Bey whether he had been given any advice about selecting a mate that would become the parent of his children and what he was told in this regard, he offered the following:

"Yes—my closest friend suggested that my wife would make a very good choice—that she would create stability in my life which was lacking at the time. She was right. My wife has been the making of me. Without her, I don't know where I would be now."

So, what advice will Mr. Bey give his son about parenting and selecting a mate that will someday become the parent of his son's children and Mr. Bey's grandchildren? What qualities will Mr. Bey tell him to look for in a mate?

"I would tell him to have patience. It is not going to come together all at once. The kids are not going to become disciplined little angels overnight. Nor will they win all the spelling bees. Children grow up just fine not being super kids who are whisked from soccer to karate to music lessons. Let the kids grow up at their own pace. Also, I would tell him that he can spare the rod and love the child at the same time. In searching for a mate, I would tell him first not to search too hard, the right mate is seldom found in the lonely heart ads or on the Internet. Find someone in environments where you can do what you love—someone with whom you have shared interests and complementary ideas. I would tell my son to be honest with himself more than anything when it comes to choosing a mate. By that, I mean don't let yourself get caught up in the moment or swept away by a pretty face or a cute figure. Many relationships fail because they are superficial. He should look for someone who is in possession of herself—some one who owns herself and who has a vision of her future. Someone who knows what she wants even if the definition of what she wanted evolved over time—at least she would be thinking and would not be carried off by the circumstances of the world. Instead, she would make circumstances that would carry her off to where she wanted to go. That's a lot for a young mind to think about and most young people don't think quite that deeply. I have tried quoting Shakespeare's Polonius, but I think that it may be a few years before his admonitions sink in."

Who were Mr. Bey's role models as he made his journey from childhood to manhood?

"Aside from the example of my parents holding down jobs and never letting us kids know how poor we were, I had the same type of role models that most kids have growing up in the Television Age—inappropriate ones. We had no Black Superman, no Black Wonder Woman. The few groups that stood out like the Black Panthers or the Nation of Islam were not touted as role models in my house. I'm too ashamed to tell you who the heroes of my youth were, but as I approached my late teens they were quickly replaced by men like Marcus Garvey and Malcolm X and women like Sojourner Truth and Ida B. Wells. My grandfather knew Marcus Garvey. Grandfather was a Major in his army and spoke about him whenever he came to visit. I rediscovered these heroes for the first time and they helped to shape my world view—a world view which included two powerful ideas—that the world was not going to devote itself to making me happy and that no man will work as hard for me as I would for myself!

"I wanted to learn about Mr. Bey's father. How had his father influenced Mr. Bey's perception of the world and his place in it?

"You are really walking on sensitive ground now," Mr. Bey responded with a wry smile. "Well, honestly, I only knew my father as my father. I did not know him as a man or what kind of life he had before I was born or what experiences he had on the job or in the Army during World War II and Korea. But it is safe to say that his experiences contributed to the person I knew. I know that he was married before and during his life—before he met my mother— he had plenty of girlfriends. His Army scrapbook is full of black and white photos of pretty girls he knew in Texas or California. Much of what I know about my father, I learned from my mother during the years that he was ill and could not speak. For one thing, he was very devoted to his family. He was known to visit his mother and aunt and to take care of their shopping or other needs. He was hard working. We never missed a meal. He insisted that we all get an education and sent all of us boys to the local Catholic School. Mother read to us and he encouraged us to do our homework. He bought us science books to fire our imaginations and encyclopedias to aid us with our homework. He was a hard disciplinarian as well and was from the 'Old School' where discipline was concerned. I can still remember many of the whippings I received for lying or being bad in some other way. To be fair, I must say that Father came from a time when Black folks were always trying to keep their kids in line as they knew what the larger world of America had in store for them, if they did not behave. His conduct towards his children had effects that are still very much with us all today. More than anything, his actions have made me a careful planner, a clear thinker and serious about getting things done."

So, in what ways does Mr. Bey feel that he is influencing his son's perspective of the world outside of his environment and his son's search for his place in it?

"I believe that I am influencing my son's perspective of the world outside of his environment and his search for his place in it by trying every now and then to inject some reality into his reality and by asking my son simple questions about his goals and how he is going to reach them and suggesting that if he wants what he says he wants, he is going to have to work for it, while keeping his head when things go wrong. I try also to inform my son about the political and economic realities of the world he lives in. I let him know that more and more, the world of the future will not care what color he is—but rather, what skills he will bring to the table."

I wanted to know if Mr. Bey thought that enough attention is being given to men's health issues including information about medical research, clinical trials and preventive health measures that exist in an effort to combat the alarming rise of heart disease, prostate cancer and diabetes experienced by men.

"No. More attention needs to be placed on these issues—the more the better," Mr. Bey said flatly.

Does Mr. Bey believe that there are adequate resources for men who are fathers, fathers-to-be and young men who are not yet fathers in the form of parenting classes and support groups? And what programs and resources would he like to see created and maintained?

"Where such programs exist they are probably doing a good job. There is always room for another mentor, another support group or parenting class particularly in high schools. Where the programs do not exist, I would like to see more real-world education in our public schools—more classes where real people—real fathers, in particular, are brought in to stave off this growing notion in America that the fathers, particularly African American fathers, are not needed. Let the young men see men in suits, lab coats and carrying briefcases, let the men be seen in uniforms and wearing tool belts or carrying a laptop—not just running around with one pants leg up, their pants down around their butts, dribbling basket balls or 'maxin' in front of 'Benzes' in music videos."

When I asked Mr. Bey to talk about the legacy he wants to leave for his child, his response was: "I want to leave a legacy of hard work and devotion to family, knowledge of and respect for self and family."

And what are Mr. Bey's aspirations for his son?

"My aspirations for my son are simply that he believes in himself and the possibilities for the future—and that he never gives up on his dreams or trades them in for security."

It seems that forty, thirty and as recent as twenty years ago, there was very little said—at least publicly—about the challenges that Men who were Fathers faced. What has changed and why are men so willing to talk openly about the challenges of parenting?

According to Mr. Bey, the value of men as fathers has changed: "The value of men as fathers has changed. The value of men as men, particularly, the value of African American men has changed. Since the days of the slaveholders until now, the image of Black men has migrated from one acceptable stereotype to another, from Zip-coon to Stepin Fetchit to Amos and Andy and finally to Irkle and Martin. Always the clown with their mouths open! We are still forced to fight the battles of our fathers—the fight for respect and acknowledgement as a necessary part of society. No longer faced with open-handed racism or Jim Crow, we as men of color, in particular, are faced with the growing perception which is created by the mainstream media that we are no good and of even less use to our own segment of society. We live in a throw-away society. It is little wonder that one day people would begin to suggest that fathers are not needed. Men are willing to talk and fatherhood is discussed so widely because men have begun to doubt themselves as much as others have. We have begun to believe the lies about ourselves to the point where we as fathers are not certain we can make a difference sometimes. While not all men are having these doubts consciously, we have been told by some women, by instant experts on television, in magazines and on the Internet that women don't need men, that children should be allowed to have their anger and not be disciplined. Men are speaking out because no one is speaking out for us. It is up to us as men to be heard and to be understood, not to be feared or hated or dismissed by those who lose nothing by denouncing us as a group."

RANDY L. COLLINS

"... MY FATHER SHOWED ME BY EXAMPLE
THE PERSON I COULD BE AND GAVE ME SAFETY
ENOUGH TO BECOME THE MAN I AM ..."

He is a poet, antiques and collectable dealer and a disability rights activist. He is RANDY L. COLLINS a resident of Fort Wayne, Indiana whose only son, Jermaine, died in October 2002 from complications due to spinocerebellar degeneration—a genetic condition that Collins shares. While he has degrees, titles and affiliations with professional associations, Mr. Collins rejects those things as defining factors. Why? He believes that those things do not factor into any discussion about Fatherhood because, in his view, Fatherhood involves all men through a divine appointment from God.

"Too often people explain who they are with their education degrees, work titles and professional associations, but these are things conferred by others—not who you really are. In other words, society likes to define people by common agreement on the value of those things achieved through educational institutions, businesses and associations," Mr. Collins explained. An independent counselor, Collins dropped out of the professional social services arena ten years ago to "freelance" his services. He felt that the social services institutions were designed to perpetuate the problem in order to continue their funding and were not really helping people improve their lives long enough to such a degree that they would no longer need their services.

I asked Mr. Collins whether he was given any advice about Fatherhood. I wanted to know who gave him the advice.

"No, I was never given any specific verbal advice about Fatherhood. It was assumed that Fatherhood was one of those natural progressions in life and was not talked about. It was part of manhood and needed no discussion. When I was the child, my parents were my elders and you were not allowed to question your elders. And as a child any other child whom I might have asked for advice would probably have been as confused as I was—not only by the question, but by the sheer audacity of my even asking it. My father was king of his household and the appointed keeper of my inheritance. He held this position by appointment of the Creator. My mother and my 17 brothers and sisters, all stood in agreement as to his rightful leadership as Father. He led by example. He clothed and fed us, made sure we received the available education, paid the bills, provided structure and rules. He loved us and disciplined us (albeit never in anger) and never missed a day's work in 40 years, with the exception of an occasional flu. As I stated, he led by example. And he was a good example. He didn't speak much. His silent glare spoke volumes. To him, words just got in the way. However, he did allow us to participate in pleasing him, which is what we all lived to do. He sometimes would allow one of us to shine his shoes. This was not a task: if it had been we would have failed miserably. We would get polish all over the place, even on our faces! He would just give a satisfied grunt, take the shoes, brush them a bit and put them on. That's all we needed to start beaming. We had pleased Daddy. Our day was complete. We were whole. I was never given any specific verbal advice about Fatherhood, but I was given an example of what kind of man I wanted to be. My first step in life was to become a man. No one told me this—they didn't have to. It was written in my being. My very essence was composed of a desire to be, to learn, to expand, to become needed and have something to give. When it is all said and done, all I ever wanted was to be a man. Therein lies the dilemma. A man is a Father—whether the children are biologically his offspring or not. Children look to him for safety, security, love, approval and esteem (things they later convert into self-esteem). A Father is a person who has delayed his own personal gratification to meet a family's needs and displays his character through a living example of sacrifice," he responded.

So, was Mr. Collins given any advice about selecting a mate that would become the parent of his children? What was he told?

"No, I was not given any advice on selecting a mate—any mate—especially one who would become the parent of my children. I must direct my answer to its implied assumption that there existed a perceived need on my part to seek advice, or that there was a perceived need on the part of someone concerned about me to give me advice. Either approach implies that I was consciously aware of the direct correlation between cause and effect, action and reaction, behavior and consequences. I had no such idea. Because of the contrived state of adolescence, I had not had access to the experiences that might have helped me shape such associations. At puberty, I did not identify myself as part of a whole, as a social entity. I saw myself as an individual of an entirely free will. I remained separate from events that happened as a consequence of exercising my individualized free will. I certainly had no idea my actions could actually change my reality. Soon after puberty, I accidentally discovered sex. It was like discovering I had power. I had no idea. I am talking about the simply profound, devastatingly wonderful idea that magically occurred to me that I could have wildly wonderfully pleasurable sex any time I wanted. It then occurred to me that no one else, especially adults, were aware of my newfound abilities, and if I just kept them secret, I could exercise my individualized free will indiscriminately. The result was a son, born when I was 17 and his mother was 16. About that, I had no idea either. It came as quite a shock. Since I had not been taught to be a responsible youth, I knew nothing of how to be a responsible adolescent in puberty, and even less about consequences. I was unable to discriminate my actions based on desired effect—just desire, nature, life, human nature—whatever you wish to call it. My natural evolution was being shaped by the circumstantial elements of my life and I felt powerless. Only I was not powerless. My life was unfolding as it should. Life is not a series of events, it is a process. And sometimes you cannot anticipate the next stage of personal development. However, since change is the only constant in reality, we must believe evolution is growth and change is ultimately good for us. Not despite, but because of the instructing law of consequence, we have freedom of choice to exercise

discrimination in our lifestyles. But we must remember that the
freedom to choose includes the option to do nothing. Either way,
evolution is a consequence of life," Mr. Collins explained.

I was curious about Mr. Collins' role models as he made his journey
from childhood to manhood. Here's what he had to say:

"I had role models. Many of them. The '60s and '70s were
turbulent times with assassinations, riots, marches, demonstrations,
protests, campus disruptions, and drugs, drugs, drugs. All in the
midst of war. As if radical ideas and radical times weren't enough,
the only Blacks seen regularly on television series were pimps,
hustlers and other sordid characters. But there will always be truth
and everybody—especially celebrities—are more than willing to
share their particular brand. I was confused back then, although I
would never have admitted it at the time. As a result, I chose to get
along with all people and adopt the best traits of everyone. I learned
humor from Richard Pryor; poise from Richard Roundtree; soul
and seduction from Isaac Hayes; fearlessness from Clint Eastwood;
spiritual faith from Earth, Wind & Fire; dignified intellectual
dissent from Malcolm X; and peace with dignity from Dr. Martin
Luther King, Jr. Not to mention President John F. Kennedy, Stevie
Wonder, Marvin Gaye and countless other people who defined
those times. Indeed, my reality was my role model and I was its
clay. Still am. It has shaped me, molded me, re-shaped me, re-
molded me again—always to improve, impossible to fail, destined
to perfection in progress. Yes, I have had many role models and
now I just want to be there for someone else."

I wanted to know about Mr. Collins' father. What is he like?
How did his father influence him and his perception of the world
and his place in it?

"My father is in his seventies," Mr. Collins stated. "Yet neither
the youthful glint in his eye nor the turn-on-a-dime gait to his
step gives a clue to his maturity. Some people have a source of
energy that seems to regenerate like clockwork. When they are
tired, they sleep. When they are reading the newspaper, they appear
to be 'scanning' while sharing their thoughts with the next project.
They are always busy, but it never appears to be work. That's Daddy.

And I admit to my lack of objectivity about him. Throughout my childhood and beyond, he always appeared to be a focused and deliberate man. He never missed a day's work at the foundry from which he retired as a foreman and I never heard him complain about having to go. I think he considered work a man's obligation for which he received dignity in return. I think the money he made was nice, but his contentment at being able to meet his obligations as a man, as well as perform his duties as a Father, garnered him respect from all who knew him. And that is like glancing at yourself as you pass the mirror, and being satisfied with what you see. It is its own reward. My father doesn't say much, so when he does speak, you know it is something important, not something you could easily learn through observing. My father is a straightforward man. Politics to him is the lie, how people treat you is the truth. He's a family man. I don't just mean his wife and kids: I mean—his sisters and brothers, cousins, aunts, uncles, you name it. Our family reunions are huge. At these reunions, I honestly can't remember who a third of the people are. But they are family and they forgive me if I can't remember all their names. The reunions are usually held in Mississippi, Milwaukee, Chicago or St. Louis, but they could be held anywhere. As a result, I have taken my role as uncle, nephew and cousin as seriously as that of husband or father. So, my perspective is that the world is my home, my home is where I live, it's a big place, and if I want to be comfortable, I must take care of it. My father showed me by example the person I could be and gave me safety enough to become the man I am. My place."

So, in what ways does Mr. Collins feel that a father should influence his children's perception of the world outside of their environment and their search for their place in it?

"My father taught me a more common-sense approach in understanding the world. He encouraged me to perceive reality as it presents itself. This practical approach allows me to observe and confirm what I perceive to be true according to my six senses. I often misinterpreted situations in the beginning. I was terribly naïve. But with the experience came refinement and a sort of fine tuning. And I began to see and accept my place in the world. To be certain, I've made my share of mistakes. But never one so big as to sacrifice my dignity to heal my wounded pride. Yeah, I've made mistakes. Probably will make a few more. But, I've learned from my father that a mistake is only a lesson in disguise. Nowadays, I find I don't have to make the whole mistake before it becomes a lesson. Yes, Fathers influence the choices of the children in their lives, especially their own. Just by being a presence. Every day. Once a week. It doesn't matter, as long as it's consistent. Someone the child can count on. All a man needs to do to be a Father is be there. It also couldn't hurt to let the child participate in age-appropriate tasks. Children love to participate with Daddy. Children are just inexperienced human beings and deserve to be considered and approached as such. Therefore, any opportunity that presents itself to communicate with a child should be handled with patience and deliberate presence of mind. Even with honor. Children are, in a very real sense, our future investment in ourselves. They will live their lives according to the character we help them shape. If what you see is what you get, then isn't it wise for us to be visionary in raising our children to become a better future for ourselves? Perhaps perception is indispensable to understanding."

When I asked Mr. Collins whether enough attention is given to men's health issues such as heart disease, diabetes and colon cancer, etc. by the media and medical and scientific communities, he offered the following:

"My answer is emphatically 'No!' In recent years, genetic science has shown us these conditions are detectable and can be monitored at an early age. Therefore, I see little reason why research and health education should be delayed until such time as it becomes necessary for crisis intervention. Awareness, health education and health maintenance should become typical aspects of our primary and secondary education institutions. I see no reason why health care should not be attached to junior high, high school and collegiate sports. If we are asking children to physically exert themselves to the point of physical endurance, and in some cases beyond, just to learn the values of competition and/or team effort, then it is socially responsible to help them maintain good health. As long as sports remain a part of the curriculum at those institutions, physical fitness, physical health, and an appropriate physical maintenance regimen should be a part of it. Because sports has become an increasingly important social institution for boys, attaching health matters to it makes sense. This should be done by men talking matter-of-factly to boys as the opportunity presents itself about health issues (kind of a 'your body: an owner's manual' approach). And by starting boys talking about their bodies and health matters at younger ages, we can change the American male culture of stoicism that prevents many men from seeking medical help at early enough stages. This health education should include such things as the routine maintenance that a man should do for his body, at what point to seek a doctor rather than 'sucking it up,' what behaviors are risky to a man's health, and how to protect your health through wise lifestyle choices. Finally, any health component attached to sports should include access to doctors through such things as routine diagnostic and maintenance testing, inoculations, dental care, etc., so that boys can get used to seeing doctors at earlier ages. Seeing yourself as a contributing agent to your own life, and therefore, identifying your responsibilities to self, creates a level of awareness that encourages responsibility. Life is a process which involves making choices all along the way— good or bad. Choices mean consequences. By becoming an active participant in the management of our lives, we will feel so empowered that it will be a great privilege to pass it on to our children."

I then asked Mr. Collins whether adequate resources existed for Men who are Fathers, Fathers-to-be and young men who are not yet Fathers. I was curious to learn about the programs and resources that he felt should be created and maintained.

"Your questions offer an opportunity to address issues at the core of the ever-changing roles Men and Fathers are asked to play," Collins stated. "A father is a man who has delayed his own personal gratification to meet the needs of a child and who displays his character through his sacrifice. Men naturally adapt to fatherhood.

It is genetically pre-programmed into us as part of the human species to sacrifice for our young. It is also pre-programmed into women. While aid and peer support are valuable assets, men have a natural aptitude to act as fathers (e.g., providers, protectors, breadwinners, etc.). That same natural attitude has been diminished by the shifting paradigm of what we today think constitutes a parent, a child, or a family, etc. No one is at fault. There is no fault. Societal norms are simply changing to reflect advances in technology. In fact, we are in the midst of social evolution driven by our booming technology. Our self-image before technology was a simple one with few choices. If you had children, you got a job, changed dreams and took care of your obligation. Today, however, social roles become more fluid with women sharing the bread-winning role and men being asked to take up more of the housekeeping and child-rearing responsibilities. Roles are now so intermixed with the options afforded us by increasing mobility that tradition has become obsolete. As a result, we're sometimes confused about our responsibilities. Sometimes we even assert our rights as a way of detaching ourselves from our responsibilities. Sometimes we may need to be reminded of our responsibilities. One resource I can recommend for single fathers, indeed single parents, is Parents Without Partners. It is not a government or social service agency program, but a social group to support singles primarily as parents. It is particularly good at supporting single and/or divorced fathers as they struggle to maintain fatherhood as the non-custodial parent. For custodial fathers, it provides a positive social outlet as well as peer support. Part of its success as a resource is that it offers a safe environment for single parents to share concerns. These parents can give each other support because most are dealing with the same issues. They provide family activities, singles activities, and children's activities. They also provide legal referrals. Single parents have often been players in an adversarial judicial system. They are usually scarred by the experience and it may take a while before normal human interactions resume. Until that happens, it may prove healing and beneficial to have a support system and understanding social outlet. Parents Without Partners is not meant to be a permanent solution to a temporary problem. Thus, the group can be approached with healing in mind. Today's world is changing. With more accessible communities, air travel, myriads of social services, and an economy almost able to regenerate at will, people can tailor their lifestyles to fit their needs. This translates into greater mobility. We no longer find ourselves bound by geography, lifestyle, earning capacity, or even lack of education. We can go anywhere, anytime, start new careers, build new families and lives. In other words, we can become serial people. Fathers will, and should, play a greater role in helping to shape their children's world. But before that, maybe we should concentrate on helping to shape the world we will ask them to share. To young men who are not yet fathers, I say: Just be a responsible person. That may not be as easy as it sounds. Being responsible means considering the consequences before you act. Not just looking at them, but actually discussing them with yourself the 'what-ifs.' For every action, there is a reaction. For every cause, there is an effect. For every piece of property, there is a deed. Ask yourself: 'Is it time for the paperwork, or am I still just playing house?'"

So, why has Fatherhood become such a widely discussed topic? Why are men so willing to talk openly about the challenges of parenting? What has changed?

According to Mr. Collins, the discussion of Fatherhood is directly linked to the changing world view on parenting: "Fatherhood has become widely discussed in response to the changing world view of what constitutes parenting. Fathers are increasingly concerned about the confusing effects of having to share the role of breadwinner with mothers. In many families, both parents work, necessitating day care or after-school programs to provide supervision of the child in the parents' absence. In this brave new world where social roles have changed as dramatically as our technology, men cannot afford to think that working mothers and strangers can perform our rightful duties as fathers. We must assert our natural right to influence and help shape the lives of our children. As the most important example in our children's lives, we have the responsibility to establish bonding relationships that provide our children with a sense of security, well-being, stability and comfort. We must become the caretakers of our children. Fundamental to our children's vision of us must be faith and safety. Men are fast becoming aware that perhaps we moved too hastily in determining custody and child support statutes. That's the dilemma. I suspect that as a society we are recognizing the need for stronger and more personal role models in the lives of young men. Girls require our attention, too, but girls seem better able to adjust to changing roles. Perhaps, we as a society put too much pressure on young men too quickly and our expectations are too high. I confess, I don't know. But those who face the dilemma should share with others what they've learned. Dialogue is good."

And what do our young men need from us as they make the journey from childhood to manhood?

"Our young men, and young women, need for us to be examples. We must consistently provide them with examples of what type of parent to become so they will be aware of the choices they may face as future parents. We must become concerned enough about parenthood to admit we have not been ideal as conscientious elders. We must become aware of, and share, the courses of life our future generations may take. One cannot give without reaching out, so we must investigate the larger world view and decide what part we want to play in it. We must then decide to reach out and share those concerns with our young—all while understanding that what they do truly matters to our future. Maslow's Hierarchy of Needs is a pyramid with each layer of development succeeding the previous layer and converging in a point at the top. This is meant to be a graphic representation of human development with each layer needing to be achieved before reaching the next layer. When the top layer is reached, it is described as having achieved 'self-actualization.' Actualize means: 'to make real, or to realize in action as a possibility.' At the bottom of the pyramid is securing the basic physical needs (e.g., food, shelter, safety, etc.) before progressing up the pyramid and on to self-actualization. Self-actualization is not an achievement, but a process of development. This is Maslow's great explanation of the process of human development. Regardless of where you find yourself on the pyramid, you are still involved in the process of self-actualization. Life is the process of striving for self-actualization. Life is also an adventure. It is impossible to predict the influences and outcomes involved in the dynamics of associating with so many different people. But life is beautiful and simple when you figure out that the only one you really have to understand is yourself. It may seem complicated. And why not? We can be complicated. But, we can also be beautiful and simple. Our lives can be filled with compassion, love, and a sense of importance and value that we share with our children. The paradigm of the world may be shifting, but this is natural and ultimately good for us. We should not resist change, but rather become more discerning about how we will allow those changes to affect us. Ultimately, it is we who are responsible for the choices we make. I trust, love, and have faith in people to respond to the world with dignity, honor, and compassion for those who are members of their family. I believe people love life and will seek any opportunity to improve it. I also believe we should share what we know with our children. Our children know nothing when they come into this world; we should, therefore, share with them everything."

LEONARD DANTZLER

"CHILDREN DON'T CARE ABOUT THE CAREER LADDER... THEY DO CARE ABOUT WHETHER OR NOT THEIR FATHER IS HOME TO EAT DINNER WITH THEM, TO TALK TO THEM... TO TUCK THEM SAFELY IN BED..."

I had an opportunity to catch up with LEONARD DANTZLER for a brief chat about parenting from a male point of view. Mr. Dantzler is an *information technology professional, a member of the Board of Directors and Chairman of the Finance Committee of the Greater Philadelphia Chapter of BDPA Information Technology Thought Leaders*—a non-profit information technology professional organization—and the father of two daughters. My conversation with Mr. Dantzler touched on a variety of issues directly and indirectly related to Fatherhood.

Was Mr. Dantzler given any advice about Fatherhood? "No," he responded. "I was not given any advice about Fatherhood. I grew up with my stepfather and we did not have the type of relationship where I would receive advice. I did not have an older brother, an uncle or any other male figure that I could look to for this guidance."

Did anyone provide Mr. Dantzler with any guidance concerning selecting a mate?

"No, I was not given any advice about selecting a mate. I didn't receive any advice from my stepfather or mother. I honestly never really thought much about this previously."

I wanted to know what Mr. Dantzler envisioned as the challenges that Men who are Fathers needed to resolve in the Millennium.

"For me personally, I believe it is the same challenge from past years which is to maintain the precarious balance of career and family. I think that this is and will probably always be the major challenge for many fathers," he remarked.

Does he feel that there are adequate resources and support systems for Men who are Fathers?

"Unfortunately, I'm personally unaware of the available resources for Fathers. This is probably because I've never really had a reason to seek out such resources, or I think that I don't need any help."

He had this to say when I asked Mr. Dantzler if there were any resources and support systems that he would like to see put in place for Men who are Fathers which he believes does not already exist: "I would like to see more organizations established to help fathers—especially young fathers become more involved in their children's lives. These organizations already exist, but the overwhelming challenge is encouraging men to actually participate in these programs."

So, what advice or key pieces of information has he given to his children or plans to give to his children about selecting a mate who will eventually be the parent of their offsprings?

"Unfortunately, I never really provided my older daughter with any advice on selecting a mate. Maybe it's because I assumed that my wife would do this or the reason could be that I didn't receive any such advice from my parents. I have the opportunity to do this with my younger daughter."

Who were his role models when he was growing up?

"My only role model was my mother. I admired her wisdom and her work ethic. She is the reason that I have confidence in myself. It was only until long after she passed away and I became a parent that I understood just how wise she was. When I was younger, I considered her my mother and father. It was not until I became a young adult and I was dealing with changes in my life that I realized something was missing. During this phase, I realized that my mother was never a complete substitute for a father, but she did the best that she could. This is all that I could ask of her," Mr. Dantzler reflected.

What are the rewarding aspects of parenting for Mr. Dantzler?

"One of the most rewarding aspects of parenting for me is to be able to come home after a long day at work and receive a hug and kiss from my daughter. At that moment every thing that occurred at work becomes an afterthought. It is a very wonderful feeling!"

And what are the most challenging aspects of parenting?

"The most challenging aspect of parenting is finding and maintaining a balance between the family and career. I failed to do this or to even recognize the importance of this with my first daughter. I hope to never make the same mistake again."

Is there an adequate focus on men's health issues (e.g., diabetes, heart diseases, hypertension, prostate cancer, etc.) in terms of research, research funding, clinical trials, and education programs by the media and the medical and scientific communities?

"I'm unsure as to whether or not there is adequate focus on men's health issues, but I do feel that the bigger issue is ensuring that men start paying attention and understanding these issues. We all know how stubborn men can be!"

Fifty, forty and even thirty years ago, there was virtually no discussion of men's issues (at least not publicly) or the need of resources and support services for Men who are Fathers. So, what in Mr. Dantzler's view, has happened or is happening in our society over the past 25 to 30 years that is resulting in a loud outcry from Men who are Fathers for support services and resources?

"I think that men have come to understand that being a father is more than going to work every day and earning money to support the family. Children don't care about the career ladder, professional titles, promotions, or the money that buys most of the things that they need or want. They do care about whether or not their father is home to eat dinner with them, to talk to them about the things that they've learned in school today, and to tuck them safely in bed," Dantzler explained.

Are we adequately equipping our young males with the tools that they will need to become successful adults—professionally and personally? Whose responsibility is it to equip our young males with the tools that they need to become successful adults—should the responsibility be shared jointly by parents, schools and churches in the community within which our young males live? Or should this responsibility be solely shouldered by the parents?

"I think that we are trying to equip our young males with the tools that they need to become successful adults, but it is not nearly enough. It would be easy to say that parents should bear the responsibility, but in reality most parents cannot do this alone. The schools, churches and other organizations within the community are all stakeholders in solving this problem," Mr. Dantzler observed.

WARREN FARRELL, Ph.D.

SANTEE, COLUMBINE . . . WHY
BOYS ARE THE WAY THEY ARE

A Columbine or a Santee makes us cry out, "What's making our children kill?" In fact, it is not our children who are killing. It is our sons.

Why? Pundits compete: "It's violence in the media." "It's the availability of handguns." "It's poor family values." But our daughters are of the same family's values, also exposed to violence in the media, also able to find the same guns in the same homes. And our daughters are not killing.

What distinguishes our sons' lives from our daughters'?

A lot. Our daughters' suicide rate is going down. Our sons' is going up. Boys and girls at the age of 9 are equally likely to commit suicide; by the age of 14, boys are twice as likely; by 19, four times as likely; by 24, six times. Each boy who kills is, in effect, also committing suicide. Both the male role and suicide are highly correlated with the repression of emotions. A Columbine or Santee may be prevented in the future by reporting boys' gun-related jokes or shadow-side fantasies. But that's only telling boys to express their feelings so we can control the feelings they express. What we repress in one place will pop up in another. Unless we care enough to be boy-sensitive at the deepest level.

For millennia societies that survived had an unconscious investment in preparing their sons for disposability in war or as workers. Unconsciously we sensed that the more our sons valued themselves as human beings, the less they would want to be disposable as human beings. Before we can find boys' inner world, we must decide what we want to emerge from their cocoon: a gun or a butterfly.

Instead, our sons are experiencing the Vietnamization of masculinity. In Vietnam, we condemned only our sons for what we drafted only our sons to do. Today our sons still see the football players being cheered for, even as we condemn their macho. The doctors and dotcommers are still considered most eligible for love, but often their focus on work and money does not make them lovable.

The Vietnamization of our sons is rewarding them for playing the old role and condemning them for having the mentality the old roles breed.

Suicide is also correlated with the failure to feel loved or needed. There is no area in which young teenage boys feel more vulnerable than in love and sex. Charles Andy Williams, the 15 year-old Santee killer, had been dating for more than a year. He had recently broken up. Boy-sensitive programs in our schools would also be sensitive to the nature of our sons' vulnerabilities in love and sex. Our daughters now have the option to initiate; our sons still have the expectation. Most boys soon learn that by the junior or senior year the more attractive girls are doing less and less of the initiating. We still say sex is dirty, and still expect our sons to initiate the dirt. Yet, when our sons know little about either girls or sex, they are expected not only to risk sexual rejection, but lectured about their penis transmitting STDs; they fear going too slowly and being a wimp or loser; or going too quickly and being a date rapist. They have most of the old role, many new expectations and very few programs focused on either encouraging our daughters to share responsibility for sexual rejection or guiding our sons through the emotional traumas induced by their old role with new demands.

Suicide is decreasing for our daughters as we increase our daughters' ways of succeeding; it is increasing for our sons as we increase our sons' ways of failing. Our schools are focused on raising the self-esteem of girls, on special programs for girls in math and science; on scholarships for females only. But it is our sons who have lower grades, are more likely to repeat a grade; are more likely to drop out; are less likely to take the SATs even if they don't drop out; are less likely to graduate from high school or college; are more likely to be in special education; have more discipline problems; who do worse in reading, writing, social studies, spelling, biology, art, languages . . . . Any parent knows that if we pay attention to one child and ignore the other, there is no question that the ignored child will act out; the only questions are how and when.

What would a boy-sensitive program look like? It would have built-in awareness of the eight signs of jeopardy Santee's Charles Andrew Williams faced. First, he is a boy; second, he is the child of divorce; third, he is living with only one parent; fourth, he is 3,000 miles away from the other parent; fifth, he rarely speaks with or sees the other parent; sixth, he is new to his school; seventh, he was dating at age 14; eighth, he recently broke up.

Good guidance begins with the guide. The Vietnamization of masculinity has produced mixed messages and confused sons. When we care as much about saving males as saving whales, we will also save ourselves. When we seek to find boys' inner world, we will give a gift to our sons in the 21st Century that we gave to our daughters in the 20th Century.

*   *   *

OUR SONS, OUR SCHOOLS

In the last third of the 20th century, feminism freed women and girls from the straight-jacket of stereotyped sex roles. No one did the same for men or boys. This is not women's fault that women cannot hear what men don't say. But it does have an impact.

Girls used to be minorities in college and graduate school. Now women are almost 60% of the full-time graduate students. They are also 54% of the full-time undergraduates and almost 70% of the part-time undergraduates.[1] In high school, girls are more likely to be in clubs, student government, on school newspapers, receive better grades, be valedictorians and salutatorians, win scholarships, and have higher professional aspirations. In contrast, they have fewer discipline problems and drop out less.[2]

This change is occurring for many reasons. Our sons are often being raised only by their mothers, then entering elementary schools with almost all female teachers. Girls have role models. Boys have gangs. Yet our daughters are still being treated like disadvantaged minorities with federal programs like "Girl Power" focusing millions of dollars on our daughters' special needs while no program focuses on our sons' special needs,

Nothing tells the story more dramatically than our sons' and daughters' suicide rates. As feminism has helped our daughters get love and respect from being whoever they want to be, our daughters' suicide rate has declined. Meanwhile, our sons' suicide rate has soared. Why? Start with the power of our children's first love. Fortunately, our daughters now have the *option* to pursue boys and take sexual initiatives. But our sons still have the *expectation*. If they do it too slowly, they are still called a wimp, but now, if they do it too awkwardly, they are sued for sexual harassment, and if they do it too quickly, they are a date rapist.

As feminism has helped our daughters have more ways to gain love and respect, it has also encouraged sexual harassment and date rape legislation that has given our sons more ways to lose love and respect. And people who feel unloved and disrespected are most vulnerable to suicide. So when our sons and daughters are nine their suicide rate is identical, but by the time they reach their early 20s, our sons' rate is six times as high.

By focusing on only our daughters, we have identified only the way our daughters experience low self-esteem and depression. So we catch our daughters' experience before it becomes suicide. Boys' experience of depression and low self-esteem is hidden in the cracks. By calling it aggression or delinquency or drinking or drugs, we skip past the depression until we stand before his coffin.

The reason boys' experience got hidden in the cracks evolved slowly over the past third of a century. It started with the shadow side of feminism—the belief that since our sons would grow up earning more money, they must have more power, privilege, and attention to their needs. We lost sight of the fact that men had been historically obligated to raise money just as women had been obligated to raise children—that obligations are not power, but, well, obligations. Roles.

We failed to see that women's attention to men's needs was conditional. Few women competed for the man reading *I'm Okay, You're Okay* in the unemployment line. It was conditional upon his willingness to earn money that often a woman would spend while he died sooner. Therefore, homeless men and gay men did not have women providing for their needs. It was conditional upon men being willing to die in war. Few beautiful princesses married conscientious objectors. Women fell in love with *The Officer And The Gentleman*, not *The Private And The Pacifist*.

Feminism helped us become aware of the price of our daughters becoming sex objects, but not the price of our sons becoming success objects. We falsely assumed that our sons' greater preparation for success meant a greater concern for who he was. We missed the fact that our sons did not become successful by learning to express who they were, but by learning to repress who they were. Successful men did not express feelings, they repressed feelings.

This is still the norm in most every American high school. The girls are most likely to fall in love with our son if he is a football player. Football players soon learn, though, that being in touch with their feelings is dysfunctional—that acknowledging his pain would lead to him leaving the game. And then the cheerleader would no longer cheer for him. She would cheer for his replaceable part.

Our sons need love and approval too much to look underneath the cheering—that her cheering is not for who he is, but for his willingness to deny his feelings. Our sons are still learning to receive love by sacrificing their bodies. But instead of calling it child abuse or prostitution, they call it "becoming a man." Or scholarship potential. Or identity. Few parents protest. Most applaud.

Our daughters have entered the Era of the Multi-Option Woman while our sons are still in the Era of the No-Option Man. Our daughters now have the option to perform, the option to pursue boys, and the option to pay; our sons still have the expectation to perform, pursue, and pay.

Our daughters are still giving their love to men who perform, and watching mothers do the same. Worldwide, two and a half billion of our daughters-as-women are still enough into the fantasy of being swept away that they were glued to Princess Diana's wedding. Few of our sons have castles to offer. When these fantasies of security become the trauma of divorce, our daughters demonize the men who failed to save them. They join First Wives' Clubs. Their fantasy of being swept away has been swept away. It is difficult for a woman who is rejected to feel a man's feelings. It is easier to label him a jerk. (It hurts less to be rejected by an object than by a full human being.) A success object who fails becomes an object of contempt and the focus of the male-bashing that is ubiquitous today.

On yet a deeper level, our sons' depression and heartaches get lost in the cracks because virtually every society had an unconscious investment in men protecting us. People who protected us had to be willing to die, not be encouraged to be in touch with their feelings. It was part of our genetic heritage, then, to select men who were killer-protectors.

Our genetic future, though, is dependent on selecting men who are nurturer-connectors. This will evolve not from a women's movement blaming men or a men's movement blaming women, but from a gender transition movement helping both sexes make a transition from following rigid roles to negotiating trade-offs in a multi-option world. For the past third of a century, we have introduced our daughters into a multi-option world; now it is time to introduce our sons.

---

[1] American Demographics, October, 1997.

[2] Michael Gurian, A Fine Young Man (Tarcher/Putnam, June, 1998).

DALE J. FRAZA

A FUNNY THING HAPPENED TO
ME ON MY WAY TO BECOMING
A HOUSE HUSBAND

Twenty years ago, my wife of thirty-five years got a promotion to property manager of the company she was working for. I was proud of her and still am. She was making twice what I was and truly loved what she was doing. At first I wasn't bothered by the money difference at all. My father was concerned and let me know it from time to time. I think he liked being able to remind me that my wife was doing better than I was. I guess he thought it would make me try harder. It didn't matter then but I guess maybe I should have tried to compete. I was selling cars for a living and kind of liked it. Unfortunately the compensation was limited and the hours were awful. I was working twenty hours a week more than she was and had very little to show for it. Three or four promotions later there wasn't any hope of catching up with her.

That's when the funny thing happened. She got pregnant with our daughter. Our son was in high school and that didn't leave us with many options. There wasn't any way she could quit working—our life style would have suffered badly. We decided that she would give birth and stay home for six weeks and then I would take over. That's when I realized that motherhood was at least twice as hard and three times more difficult than any thing I'd ever done in my life. I spent my days trying to get caught up and my nights wondering if I'd ever get any sleep again. When she was old enough for a babysitter I decided to go back to work. But in the eighties and early nineties men weren't supposed to have flexible schedules. So I tried a lot of different jobs to be able to work around my daughter's needs—exactly what most women in this country do every day. But I wasn't a woman and employers didn't care what time the babysitter had to leave. The whole thing was a process of resigning myself to the fact that I was going to have to learn to make the best out of what was left of my life. I thought once she goes to school, I'll get started again. Fat chance. No one told me about dance classes and gymnastics—never mind after school programs and sleepovers. I kind of enjoyed grade school but by the time she got into middle school I was washed up—no longer necessary. Almost all of her questions were for her mom. Of course, in high school both her mother and I were taboo.

I was in my mid-thirties when she was born and after eighteen years of short-term employment and living my life around my daughter, I found myself wanting another child. I'm not sure why, but for a long time now I've felt empty. She's a senior in college now and I kind of got my wish. I'm home taking care of my mother after a quintuplet bypass and countless other problems, wondering what happened to my life. I've taken up writing now but as you can see I should have gotten a day job. I'm in my late fifties now and wondering every day how the years passed me by without my noticing. My wife has given up on me. She tells her friends that I'm retired. I'm sure she's disappointed in the way things turned out for me and I'm not so sure she's wrong. Once in a while I go online looking for a job, but the thought of trying to explain on a resume what I've been doing for the last twenty years leaves something to be desired.

I thought there must be a support group out there somewhere for people like me but it turns out most of the women in the world have the same problems I have and they don't seem to need such a group. I know what you're thinking—I will try to get a life.

THOMAS R. GOLDEN, LCSW

MAKING A BOX—MY FATHER'S DEATH

My father died in November of 1994. During the week of his funeral my brother and I decided to design and construct the container for my father's ashes. That week, my brother Joel, and I spent time in my parents' garage, which had doubled as my father's workshop, planning and constructing his memorial container.

During this time the men who came to visit our family tended to be drawn to the workshop, while the women who visited were more likely to spend time talking inside. The men who visited usually had ideas or comments about the work that was being done, and they gladly chipped in, and did this or that to aid in the project. These gender boundaries were not solid, though. We men spent plenty of time in the house talking with visitors about my father and what he meant to us, and the women would sometimes boldly venture into the workshop area. It was not that the men and women were separated, it was that the men and women tended to have different paths to connect them with their grief.

Just as the tears flowed inside the house, they flowed in the workshop. As we worked we would share stories about my father. One of the most important parts of this experience was the presence of my father's 80 year old best friend, Charlie Beamen. Charlie, a retired minister, was also my father's woodworking buddy. As the three of us worked together we exchanged numerous stories. Joel and I told Charlie of our days with Dad growing up, and Charlie told us of his exploits with my father in the recent past. As we worked and told stories, the tears and laughter flowed.

We men had found a safe place to act as a "container" for our emotions. The workshop functioned in this manner to connect our pain and tears with an activity. The activity of building the memorial container became a "hook" for our pain. It seemed easier, as a man, to connect with my grief through an activity rather than by simply "sharing" it. The women, I noticed, appeared to have great skill in simply sharing their grief. They were more drawn to connecting their pain, tears, and grief on a verbal level with their most intimate friends and family.

In doing further research into the bereavement process, I learned that my experience reflected the differences men and women have in the grief process. This difference puts men in a precarious state in our culture because almost all of the "action" activities related to death have been sub-contracted. Activities such as building the coffin, directing the ritual, digging the grave, or the funeral itself have been turned over to the "death professionals." This leaves men with nothing to do following a death and thereby negates many men's strength of action.

Evidence supporting these observations can be found in looking at tribal cultures and the ways they separate the tasks and roles of men and women following a death. For example, the Bara people in Madagascar literally separate the men and women. Two huts are designated: the "male hut" for the men and the "house of tears" for the women. The house of tears is the center of emotional expression, while the male hut is more the center of activities such as directing the ritual. In Australia the men of the Yolngu sing sacred songs around the bed of the person who is ill, and if death occurs, the songs continue as a means of orienting the newly dead to the Ancestors. It is said that the women join in the song with their crying and keening and the blend creates a sound of great beauty.

The Dagura men of Africa dance out their grief for the person who died. In a different African tribe the men will approach the women who are actively crying and keening and stand silently next to them. The men do this to use the women's grief as a hook, that is, as a way to ignite and resonate their own pain. This action is similar to that of a tuning fork. If one tuning fork is struck close to another one that is still, the still tuning fork will begin to resonate with the same vibration of its active neighbor. By standing near the actively grieving women the men start to get in touch with their own pain. In other cultures, the men sing the life of the person who died.

There are many more examples of the separate, but complementary tasks of mourning assigned to men and women in different cultures. The point here is that the men are usually given active tasks following a death and these tasks become "hooks" to facilitate a connection to their pain. Once the pain is "hooked," it can be expressed and released which brings us one step closer to healing.

In our own culture there are also examples of men who use a task or activity to connect to their emotional pain. Eric Clapton wrote a song about his child who died. Through his strength of music Clapton has found a way to honor his pain by creating a song about his son.

Abraham Lincoln is said to have had a habit of inviting a male friend to the White House to play what Lincoln called "sad songs." This man and Lincoln would walk silently to a room in the White House and the man would sit at the piano and play the songs. As he played Lincoln would sit and cry. The songs were Lincoln's hooks to enter his state of grief.

Other examples include the AIDS Quilt, all of the memorials in Washington, D.C., and a memorial World Wide Web site, such as the one I created as part of my work in the area of grief. All of these examples provide people with activities which allow a connection to their pain by actively honoring the person who died. This can be a powerful healing IF the activity is connected with the pain. If not connected to the pain, it is merely a hollow exercise.

While men and women have different strengths and needs in their healing process, these needs are often complementary and overlapping. As our culture finds it difficult to recognize and hold the pain that comes with loss, members of both sexes often find themselves in a difficult place when it comes to grief. We need more culturally endorsed "active" rituals that give us "hooks" into our grief. By becoming aware of the differences we have in our own chosen style of grief and healing, we are in a better position to find our own hooks and honor those around us and ourselves.

L.T. HENRY

LETTERS TO MY SON

Dear Son,

There are a few basic pieces of knowledge
that would have helped me a great deal.
Like, how to pick the right mate.
It is better to get as much information
as you can concerning Fatherhood.
Are you ready?
If not, why?
Protect yourself until you are ready.
There will be emotional decisions.
There will be intellectual decisions.
Usually, you will find what is best for you
when these two parts of you are in line.

Love,

Dad

Dear Son,

A Father should try to lead by
becoming his child's first hero.
Fathers should be teachers of the next generations.

Love,

Dad

Dear Son,

The basic question to ask about Fatherhood is:
"How will you take care of your child?"
Yes, it is true that minutes of passion can
change the direction of your life forever.
Try to become friends first, before you become sex partners.

Love,

Dad

Dear Son,

Never lose your sense of humor.
And if you don't have one, find one.
Don't take yourself too seriously.
If you gain a sense of humor,
you will not carry a lot of negative baggage with you
and it will lead you to better decisions.

Love,

Dad

Dear Son,

It's best not to look for quick answers to problems.
Put yourself in a never ending search for truth.

Love,

Dad

Dear Son,

Beware of the profilers.
These are people who do things for image.
Not for love or compassion.

Love,

Dad

Dear Son,

Be wise in Life.
Never listen to a person unless their body language
and every thing about them emanates what they are saying.
People will look at you and say, "I am happy. I am joyous."
And their body language will say something entirely different.
When people speak, two things have to be together—
their mind and their body language.
If these two things are together, feel comfortable.
If these two things are not together, then distrust
what they are saying.

Love,

Dad

Dear Son,

When it comes to raising children,
you will find that "instant success" does not exist.
Do your homework.
Build a solid foundation.
There are many things to learn.

Love,

Dad

Dear Son,

You are only in competition with yourself.
Make every day better than the day before.

Love,

Dad

Dear Son,

There are no excuses for Success.
Only for Failure.

Love,

Dad

Dear Son,

We all have a responsibility to overcome our environment
and the set of circumstances we are born into.

Love,

Dad

Dear Son,

It is always important to know
how you feel and what you think.
And it is equally important to know
what others think and how they feel.

Love,

Dad

Dear Son,

Everybody makes mistakes.
The tragedy lies in not learning anything from them.

Love,

Dad

Dear Son,

Learn to make your own plan.

Love,

Dad

Dear Son,

What you think and what you say can
impact greatly upon others.
Examine your thoughts.
Choose your words carefully.

Love,

Dad

Dear Son,

The more you know,
the more you will find out what you do not know.

Love,

Dad

Dear Son,

It's easy to find a Thinker.
A Thinker never stays in the same place mentally.

Love,

Dad

MY SON'S LIFE

I would like to say a few words
about My Son's Life.
Now, I could talk to you
about all of my son's weaknesses;
but that would only be the person
that you thought you saw.
I'm here today to talk about a genius
that walked among us,
talked among us,
and played his music among us.
There are many things that geniuses
have in common.
They don't think like we do.
It takes a different mind
to hear music where there are no notes.
It takes a different mind to create a song
where there are no words.
Most geniuses live lives of agony
and tumult and lives
that we cannot understand.
Maybe we are not supposed to understand.
Maybe we are supposed to remember
the songs that geniuses create
and the music that they have played.

FOR MY SON

TOMMY

OCTOBER 24, 1962   MAY 25, 1987

© 26 MAY 1987

THOMAS HOERNER

A DIALOGUE WITH "AMERICA'S SINGLE PARENTING GURU"

His humorously informative book—*The Ultimate Survival Guide For The Single Father*—has caused some to call him "America's Single Parenting Guru" and "The King Of Guy Talk On Running A Household." THOMAS HOERNER is a man who is going places. He possesses a disarming sense of humor and manages to balance, with great agility, his roles as a custodial parent of three sons, author, and Executive Liaison for Fathers for Equal Rights, Inc. in Dallas, Texas.

"I'm a forty-five year old and have custody of my three sons. At the time I took custody, my youngest was three and today, my oldest is twenty-one. In that time, I've earned a 'B.S.' degree from the Home Institute of Domestic Engineering and Family Development Center. I specialize in balancing a career, home, family and a social calendar. I have three well-rounded children, a successful career, a good co-parenting relationship with my ex-wife and a healthy personal life. I thought I could write a book, sell a million copies and retire at forty-five," Mr. Hoerner responded when I asked him to talk about himself.

I wanted to know if Mr. Hoerner had been given any advice about Fatherhood. I was curious to know what he was told and who told him.

"I was scared about being a father for the first time and told my mother that I didn't know if I had what it takes to be a father. She said, 'Don't worry. Kids are like pets that love back. Treat them like your dog and you'll have it made.' To this day, my kids hate it when I whistle for them!" Mr. Hoerner quipped.

When I asked Mr. Hoerner if he was given any advice about selecting a mate, he responded: "It's just as easy to love rich as it is to love poor."

Of course, I asked the obvious. Who supplied Mr. Hoerner with this interesting piece of advice?

"Russ—my best friend who married a CEO who lost her job when her company went bankrupt!"

The conversation turned to Fatherhood in the Millennium. I asked Mr. Hoerner to discuss the challenges that Men who are Fathers in the Millennium face and must resolve.

"Equality in health and as parents," came the answer. "Men die six years earlier than women. We spend ninety million dollars on breast cancer research and less than ten million dollars on prostate cancer. Men are not looked at as parents. We are paychecks. That's why women have no problem finding help collecting support, but men have no where to go for help enforcing visitation."

Are there adequate resources and support systems for Men who are Fathers?

"No! There are no shelters, no legal aid, no federal funding for fathers' groups and very little effort to help young men become contributing fathers. There are always problems helping fathers solve support problems. There should be a way to confirm arrearages or settle disputes fast, easy and with no cost—without tying up our court system. There should also be help adjusting support due to unemployment and disabilities."

And what advice does Mr. Hoerner plan to give to his children about parenting and raising children?

"Never use a pacifier. Don't give your son your name. Start saving for college at birth and teach respect, honesty and compassion for others."

When I asked Mr. Hoerner if there were any key pieces of information that he planned to share with his children about selecting a mate who would eventually become the parent of their offspring, he offered the following: "Looks are temporary. But, if you want to know what your wife will look like thirty years from now, look at her mom. You better make sure you like the person."

So, who were Mr. Hoerner's role models during his formative years?

"My father. He never yelled or used domestic violence. That was quite an accomplishment with the trouble I caused. Domestic violence is learned at home. Hit your kids and you will teach them to solve problems in the same manner," he remarked.

What are the most rewarding aspects of parenting for Mr. Hoerner?

"Hearing 'Dad, I love you!' has always been at the top of my list. But watching my children graduate from high school runs a tight second. Something about that major step to adulthood put a tear in my eye and made a deposit in the 'Proud To Be A Dad Bank'," he responded.

And what are the most challenging aspects of parenting for Mr. Hoerner?

"Staying consistent with restrictions. I hate to see my children unhappy, so I give in too easy when it comes to enforcing punishments."

GARY A. JOHNSON

"PARENTING IS A SERIOUS JOB THAT REQUIRES
UNENDING SACRIFICE, PATIENCE AND
COMMITMENT."

He is the Founder and Editor-in-Chief of Black Men In America.com, a highly acclaimed online magazine for African American men, and the creator of a cyberspace forum for women called "Women Sound Off." Through the Gary A. Johnson Company located in Temple Hills, Maryland, he provides consulting services in the areas of multicultural management, harassment prevention and facilitation. He has developed an awarding winning website—Gary's Homework Help Page—which has been lauded by USA Today Education and NBCi as one of the best homework help web sites on the Internet. He is GARY A. JOHNSON—a man who has become all things to all people outside of his family circle.

Mr. Johnson describes himself as being an "ordinary man trying to do some extraordinary things." Did he receive any advice about Fatherhood?

"You bet!" Mr. Johnson responded. "I was given advice about Fatherhood from my father and mother. They told me not to be a father until I was ready to be responsible and make the necessary commitment. They also cautioned me that if I was irresponsible that I could possibly ruin the lives of other people. That always stuck with me. Separately, my mother told me that being a good parent requires patience and sacrifice. My father wasn't much of a talker on those subjects. He essentially led by example. All I had to do was watch how he treated our family, including my mother, grandparents and the extended family members that lived with us when I was growing up. His actions spoke louder than any words that I could hear at that time."

Did Mr. Johnson receive any advice about selecting a mate. What was he told? Who told him?

"I was given plenty of advice on selecting a mate. My father,

Samuel Johnson, was my 'Best Man' when I got married. He shared several pieces of advice with me that have helped me in my 17 years of marriage." His father's "pearls of wisdom" included the following:

- All you need in life is one good friend.
- Never start anything in a relationship that you're not willing to keep doing or maintain
- When you get married, listen to your wife and do what you have to do to maintain the relationship. If you and your wife run your household a certain way, then you work with her—not your buddies. Don't take the advice of your friends over the advice of your wife.
- If your wife sends you to the store to buy Tampons, then go to the store and buy Tampons. Do what you have to do to keep your household intact.
- Never embarrass your partner in public and keep certain things between the two of you and not in the street.
- Never put your hands on a woman in anger. If you get mad or upset, leave the house or go for a walk.

When asked to identify what he believes are the challenges of Fatherhood in the Millennium, Mr. Johnson offered the following:

"Wow, that's a tough question. I think maintaining and passing on values to our young people. Values, in terms of respect, honesty, hard work and decency. There are very few shortcuts that pay off, especially for Black folks. I have two sons and I try to teach them values. From the time my sons could talk, I started teaching them to think and reason. That's so important. When they got in trouble and would try to explain things, I would give them credit if they employed some kind of thinking process. They still got in trouble, but the punishment was not as harsh. I would really get upset if they didn't think or use any logic at all," he remarked. "When they were little boys I taught them how to look people in the eye when they talked to people, to hold the door open for people, and to say 'please' and 'thank you.' Also, I think education is a major challenge for the millennium. Generally speaking, I think the bar has been lowered in terms of educating children in schools, both public and private schools. If parents don't get involved with what's going on in their child's school and hold some of these teachers and administrators accountable, our children will suffer and will not be prepared to compete for jobs when they leave school."

The discussion moved to whether or not there are adequate resources and support systems for Men who are Fathers.

"No, I don't think that there are enough resources. I also think that in some cases where there are resources, those resources are mismanaged. Again, I come back to education. Many folks aren't aware of the resources that are available to them and others who do know of resources, for a variety of reasons, don't take advantage of the opportunities."

Are there any resources or support systems that, in Mr. Johnson's view, do not exist that he would like to see put into place for Men who are Fathers?

"This is a difficult question for me to answer because I'm not as knowledgeable in the area of support systems and resources that are available for men who are fathers. I've always had the support of my family and extended family," Mr. Johnson stated

So, how does Mr. Johnson, as a Father and entrepreneur, whose work takes him away from home, maintain an active and dominant role in his children's lives? Here's what he had to say:

"I have a management and consulting business that I've run for eight years. Two years ago, I got into the web business and launched *Black Men In America.com,* which many say is the premier online magazine for Black men. The decision to quit my job has already paid huge dividends for my family and me. The quality of all of our lives has improved. I'm able to maintain an active and dominant role in my children's lives because I made it my primary focus from Day One. From the time my sons were born, I've always taken them everywhere with me. I would take them to the grocery store, the hardware store, to the mall, you name it, and they were with me. Again, I have to come back to the support of my wife. Without her support, I'd probably be divorced, still working my 9 to 5 job or both. I've also been blessed with a supportive family. My family and my wife's family, including our sisters, all live within 20 minutes of each other. Our families get along. How many couples can boast that their parents and in-laws vacation together and take the kids? Now that's a blessing that I don't take for granted. I also arranged my management and consulting business so that I could work from home or my office, which is about 15 minutes away from home. In addition, I make my business trips as short as possible. I deliver seminars for a living and I have the flexibility of structuring my schedule so that I'm not away from home for long periods of time."

At one point, Mr. Johnson decided to stay home with his children and in the process temporarily put his career on hold. I wanted to know why. What were and are the benefits of his willingness to become a dominant presence in his children's lives for a certain length of time by virtue of the fact that he was physically present in the home? Did his decision to stay at home with his children come at a critical point in their intellectual, emotional and physical development?

"By all accounts I had a great career in the federal government. I was on the 'fast-track' and well regarded. However, I felt that something was missing. So I quit my job and took advantage of an early retirement incentive package at the age of 36 and stayed home with my two young sons. I had the support of my wife, a viable game plan and stepped out on faith. My sons were 4 and 7 years old. I have never ever regretted the decision to quit my job. The main benefit of my being physically in the home is the personal interaction that I have with my kids on a daily basis. Simple things like talking with them in the car on the way to school or laughing at bath time are priceless memories. In the case of my youngest son who is now 12, he can't remember a time when I was not home. In his world, Dad has always been around to take him to school, ball practice and anywhere else he needed to go. When I moved into office space, I took my youngest son shopping with me to pick out office furniture. Part of the office furniture was a new desk and chair for him. Sometimes I take him to the office after school and he can do his homework while I work. I also bought a video game system so my young men can have some fun. I try to incorporate my boys into almost every aspect of my life. I remember some advice that an older co-worker told me before I quit my job. This guy was old enough to be my father. He said, 'Gary, you do what you have to do. If you miss this time with your kids, you can never get it back. I didn't take advantage of the opportunity to spend time with my kids and I regret it to this day.' From that day on I always strived for *balance* and *stability*. Quitting my job gave me the luxury of being able to be at my children's school and develop relationships with their teachers. I also have the flexibility to ensure that homework is done and attend any extracurricular activities. My sons always had the security of knowing that their mother and father would always be there for them."

So, what advice or key pieces of information should Men who are Fathers pass on to their children about parenting, selecting a mate and male-female relationships?

"Parenting is a serious job that requires unending sacrifice, patience and commitment," Mr. Johnson explained. "Men need to select a mate that they respect and in most cases, someone that they have something in common with. Relationships last longer if they are built on a solid foundation in the form of mutual respect and friendship. I think there's something to be said for having a mate or a partner with a similar background as yours. That's not to say that couples with opposite backgrounds can't be successful, but I think the odds are more in your favor if you select someone whose background is similar to yours. For other advice, I refer you to the advice that my father shared with me which I discussed in detail earlier."

So, who were Mr. Johnson's role models as he made the journey from childhood to manhood?

"This is easy," Mr. Johnson stated enthusiastically. "My father, Sam Johnson and my grandfather Solomon Gary were my role models. When I was growing up, my father was a janitor who at one time worked three jobs. Our family car was a taxicab and yet he always managed to somehow work things out with my mother so that my sister and I felt comfortable and secure. He was the best man at my wedding and when I need advice he's the first person that I call. My grandfather only had a second grade education, and was probably the smartest man that I've ever known because he seemed to know where all the smart people were and how to use their knowledge to his advantage."

In Mr. Johnson's view, is there an adequate focus on men's health issues—diabetes, heart disease, hypertension, prostate cancer, etc.— in terms of research, research funding, clinical trials and education programs by the media and the medical and scientific communities?

"I know there's a lot of data available for men's health issues. I think the challenge is this: How do we make that data more accessible to the black community? Another challenge is combating the 'cultural conditioning' of men not to seek medical help at the first sign of trouble. Early detection is the key. A lot of brothers have their heads in the sand when it comes to their health. We need to educate our folk early and take away the negative stigma."

I noted that fifty, forty or even thirty years ago, there was virtually no discussion of men's issues—at least not publicly—or the need of resources and support services for Men who are Fathers. So I wanted to know, what, in Mr. Johnson's view, has happened in our society over the past 25 to 30 years that is causing a loud outcry from Men who are Fathers for support services and resources.

"Again, I'm no expert, but the Internet, and the advances of technology—computers, television, radio, and other mass media—have certainly made a difference. I also think that people are coming back to the 'common sense' reality that men play a key role in the overall development of their children. Is it necessary to have a man in your life to raise good kids? Absolutely not, but it sure does help. A number of women and men successfully raise their children by themselves. However, I think men, who are involved in their children's lives, become a key part of their growth and development," he explained.

I had to ask Mr. Johnson one more question. I wanted to know if he feels that we are adequately equipping our young males with the tools that they will need to become successful adults— professionally and personally. Exactly whose responsibility is it to equip our young males with the tools that they need to become successful adults?

Should the responsibility be shared jointly by parents, schools and churches in the community within which our young males live? Or should this responsibility be solely shouldered by the parents?

"You asked some excellent questions," Mr. Johnson replied. "Generally speaking, I don't think that we're equipping our young men with the tools that they need to become successful adults which I think is the same as being a good citizen. I don't think enough children are taught how to think and reason. There are fewer role models for young people and the demands on parents are more challenging than they were 30 years ago. I think all of us are responsible and should play a role to help young men get what they need to develop. When I say all of us, I mean parents, aunts, uncles, cousins, schools, churches, neighbors and friends. We just have to do it—or it won't get done. It would be nice if the parents could be responsible for raising their children, but the reality is that some parents are dysfunctional misfits who are simply bad citizens, bad examples and horrible role models. It's no secret that some of these parents are not equipped to teach their children anything of value and in some cases the children are better off without the parents. As a nation, I think we could take better care of our children. Some of the things that happen to our children qualify as criminal in my view. Child abuse, poor education in the form of schools, bureaucracy in some of the agencies that are supposed to be protecting kids could all be better. I believe that one person can make a difference—and I'm not just referring to financial resources or money. I try to touch someone in a positive way every day, either personally or through BlackMenInAmerica.com. I see myself as an ordinary man, trying to do extraordinary things."

JAMES KENNEDY

FATHERHOOD AND THE "HIP HOP" GENERATION

He is a musician, lyricist (M1), composer, producer, arranger, photojournalist, videographer, the President and Chief Executive Officer of two entertainment companies—M1 Entertainment and Oyster Shell Publishing Company, a member of the "Hip Hop" Generation and a Father. He is JAMES KENNEDY—a Man who is a Father who has become "all things to all people" outside of his family circle.

When I asked Mr. Kennedy to talk about the role models who influenced him as he made his journey from childhood to manhood, he quickly pointed to his brother—the late Gary 'Greatness' Kennedy, 'The King Of Pop'—Michael Jackson, Marvin Gaye, Run DMC, Rakim and Eric B. and KRS 1.

Why?

"Michael Jackson because of his electrifying entertainment skills. Marvin Gaye because he had a resonance within his music. Run DMC for being a trend setter. Rakim and Eric B. for some of the lyrics in their songs and contributions to Hip-Hop. KRS 1 for sacrificing himself for others. And my brother Gary who was the greatest MC that I've encountered—lyrically he had no boundaries for his talent and that's what made me what I am and I know that," the Philadelphia native explained.

I then explored with Mr. Kennedy whether he had received any advice as a young male about selecting a mate and where the advice came from.

"Yes, I was given advice about selecting a mate. My father said, 'Try not to scorn a woman'. And my mother told me, 'Love women for who they are and not what they have to give'," he responded.

The conversation then moved to whether Mr. Kennedy was

told what would be expected of him once he became a Father. Did he receive information concerning what his responsibilities would be? Who provided him with this information?

Kennedy, whose birth father did not play an active role in his nurturing and development, credits his concepts and knowledge about the expectations and responsibilities of Fatherhood to the "Talking-the-Talk-and-Walking-the-Walk School of Fatherhood" that was conducted on a daily basis by his stepfather, Mr. Oscar Bucholtz.

"I would have to say that I was *shown* more than *told* about the expectations and responsibilities of Fatherhood by the only Father I know—Mr. Oscar Bucholtz. He truly fathered my two older brothers and I and that was very important in the development of who I am. I have to give credit where credit is due. Pretty much, I learned from his example about what the responsibilities and expectations of Fatherhood would be. I think that's the best teacher," Kennedy reminisced.

So, what type of information should we share with our young males to prepare them for Manhood and Fatherhood?

"There are two things that we need to tell our young males about the responsibilities of Manhood and Fatherhood. The first thing we need to tell them is that the responsibilities of Fatherhood and Manhood are more than about money. And the second thing that we need to tell our young males deals with the responsibility of teaching our children about balance—the balance of good, bad, right, wrong, up, down and so on. In other words, the balance of contrast," he advised.

Cognizant of the fact that Mr. Kennedy's generation is referred to as the "Hip Hop Generation," I asked him to discuss the challenges and pressures that he faces on a day-to-day basis as he nurtures, loves and mentors his children. I wanted to know how he, as a Father from the "Hip Hop Generation," dealt with these pressures and challenges. For Kennedy, the pressures and challenges that he faces on a day-to-day basis as he nurtures, loves and mentors his children has become one of the catalysts for his creative projects. He channels the pressures and challenges that he faces into lyrics and beats that are components of the creative projects which his two entertainment companies—M1 Entertainment and Oyster Shell Publishing—produce.

"My creativity is the outlet for these challenges and pressures. The challenges and pressures that I face as a Father create my raw moods which makes me write raw materials. One of the challenges that I face as a Father is spending enough time with my children. This is a challenge that I have handled by involving my children in my work. They are around me constantly—even while I am creating and producing music. As a result, my children and I—my twins and my son—have a very close relationship. My children play a significant role in the production of my music. In their own way, they assist me with the editing and marketing aspects of making music. You know, children are going to be completely honest—no matter what. I will ask their opinions about the creative projects that I work on. I will let them listen to the material that I have created. When my children start 'jamming'—when they start dancing to a beat that I've created or singing along with the lyrics, I know that it—the music—is right. I always have my kids passing through. They are truthful sounding boards. If it's right, they'll tell me. If it's not right, they will tell me that, too!"

Are there enough resources and support services for Men who are Fathers? Are there any particular needs and issues that Men from the "Hip Hop Generation" who are Fathers possess which require special attention and are not being looked at?

Mr. Kennedy says "No!"

"There are definitely not enough resources and support services. It feels as if 'somebody up top' has got it in for Men. You know, some of us know about our egotistic disorder. When I talk about an egotistic disorder, I'm talking about the fact that sometimes Men stick their chest out too far so that they hurt their back—philosophically speaking," he explains with a wry smile.

So, what are the needs of Men who are Fathers from the "Hip Hop Generation"?

"Well, I would say, that the 'Hip Hop Generation' was always into history through our sampling of music from the past. So, really, in my view, all that we need to be taught is an appreciation of a professional environment. But how can we appreciate a professional environment when we are not provided with one or taught about what a professional environment is and how to appreciate it? You know, the two generations that came immediately before the 'Hip Hop Generation' need to step out of their worlds and step into our world and we—the 'Hip Hop Generation'— need to step out of our world and step into the worlds of the two generations that have come before us. There needs to be some type of forum between the 'Hip Hop Generation' and the two generations that preceded the 'Hip Hop Generation'. The message that the 'Hip Hop Generation' is putting out to the two generations that preceded us is simply this, 'Teach us! Show us!'"

I decided to "push the envelope" and asked Mr. Kennedy whether he felt that the generation immediately ahead of his generation had adequately provided the "Hip Hop Generation" with the tools that his generation will need to succeed in a global market place. What is it that the "Hip Hop Generation" feels it needs from the generation that immediately precedes it?

Kennedy had this to say: "Well, let's talk about the first part of your question. I think that the generation before us—taught what it knew to teach. And what it knew to teach was what was taught to it. So, you can only use what was given to you. In other words, if there is any thing that is 'messed up' in any thing that you taught us, it ain't your fault. Now, let's deal with the second part of your question. What do we need from the generation that immediately preceded us? Most of all—'nonjudgment.' Don't judge us. Just understand and respect our present level of perception. The development and forward movement of our present perception level will come with time and experience. What's good for some folks may not be good for other folks. Everybody has their times of uncertainty, their times of vagueness, and just 'following' and not being completely a leader. Respect our perception level. Remember how you were when you were coming up."

What should we do to make sure that our young males possess marketable skills that will enable them to successfully compete in the global marketplace?

Kennedy offered the following advice: "You can allow us to accept whatever we are—whenever we are—until times have changed. I think that there is a freedom in that which allows you to see things much clearer and learn much quicker."

Inevitably, when issues directly and indirectly related to Fatherhood are discussed, the thorny terrain of male and female relationships is also explored. Kennedy does not shy away from the fact that his latest creative project, "Getto Born" focuses on parenting and paternity issues which take the intense dialogue on male and female relationships to the next level.

So, exactly what is the message that Kennedy is attempting to convey through "Getto Born"?

"'Getto Born' simply says to folks, 'Hey, no matter who, what or where you come from, there is always room for potential. There is always grounds for potential!'"

Mr. Kennedy shared with us the advice that he plans to dispense to his children about selecting a mate and parenting:

"First, when it comes to selecting a mate, know what you need and want and can tolerate before 'locking in.' Second, in connection with parenting, be as real as you can with your children without disrespecting their childhood development. You don't want to give your children too much information—too fast and too soon."

I asked Mr. Kennedy to explain what he would like the world to know about his generation—the "Hip Hop Generation." What is its legacy? What is its message?

"That's easy," Kennedy buoyantly responded. "The 'Hip Hop Generation' is the generation that *can make—and does make— even dirt look and sound like gold.* We can take 'nothing' and turn it into 'something.' We are working from little or nothing, but despite that, we are able to transform our dreams and visions into realities that the rest of the world can see, hear, feel and touch."

THOMAS LESSMAN

THE MILLION DADS MARCH 2003:
A CELEBRATION AND A CALL TO ACTION

He is the Founder and Chairman of the Million Dads March or "MDM" which is headquartered in Kansas in the United States. He is the man who orchestrated a worldwide gathering of Men who are Fathers on Sunday, 15 June 2003 as they engaged in a celebration of Fatherhood and a protest against the causes of the breakdown of the family. He is THOMAS LESSMAN.

I asked Mr. Lessman to describe his role in the MDM—as it related to the event's conception and the implementation of strategies that culminated in Men who are Fathers throughout our global village celebrating Fatherhood on Sunday, 15 June 2003.

"As Founder and Chairman of the MDM, my role includes a little bit of everything from enlisting leaders of the movement to drafting and implementing strategies for success. As Chairman, one of my most important functions is to be the webmaster for the MDM website (*www.MillionDadsMarch.org*). The website is an important function of the organization. It's where people get the most information about the Marches as well as what they can do to help. Being the Chairman also puts me in the position of putting myself in the line of fire from feminists and others who are hostile to our cause of Equal Parenting. I also catch a lot of flack from people within the fathers' movement who are more content to complain than to actually participate and DO something. It's not an easy job but somebody has to do it!" Mr. Lessman explained.

So, what triggered such a dramatic and unprecedented move on the part of Men who are Fathers throughout our global village to take to the streets on Father's Day—Sunday, 15 June 2003—in celebration of Fatherhood and in protest against the causes of the breakdown of the family?

"The 'trigger' is over thirty years of misandry—male bashing—
and inequality in their families. Many men are now finding out
firsthand that, in divorce or separation proceedings, they are forced
into a very unequal situation. When you live your entire life
believing in a system, only to find that the system readily destroys
you for its own gain, it hits you like a ton of bricks. Some people
turn to violence or self-pity. We prefer the more direct, non-violent
approach. Civil disobedience and public protesting go a lot further
than violence or self-destruction! Many groups are openly
advocating violence or self-destruction—such as hunger strikes,"
Lessman responded.

I asked Mr. Lessman to discuss the challenges and issues
confronted by Men who are Fathers in the Millennium. Has
the Million Dads March drawn attention to these challenges
and issues?

"Men and Fathers face dramatic challenges in order to restore
equality to their lives. Hostility from feminists and the family law
system must be defeated. Apathy must be overcome, both within
themselves and from the general public. The apathy is the worst
part currently. Until men and fathers can learn to stand up for
themselves, we cannot overcome those hostile to equality. The
Million Dads March is providing for those men and fathers—as
well as the people who support them—a platform in which they
can air their grievances and actively work to bring about peaceful
change. One of the most important challenges is our lack of
resources. While feminist organizations such as the National
Organization for Women receive tons of funding from government
and private sources, fathers' groups receive none. We have to rely
on ourselves. This is where networking plays its part. The power of
networking cannot be underestimated! As individuals or small
groups working alone, we have no chance of success. However,
working together and helping each other gives us the strength we
need in order to survive and succeed. With this in mind we work
with groups not only across the United States, but also in the
United Kingdom, Canada, Israel, Jamaica and other nations,"
Lessman remarked.

When I asked Mr. Lessman whether the Million Dads March would help to address the needs of Men who are Fathers in terms of creating and insuring that resources and support services and information concerning resources and support services reach Men who are Fathers from all Walks of Life, he had this to say:

"As far as creating resources and services, the Million Dads March recognizes that some of these services are already in place. Instead of creating new ones, we work to bring attention to those already in place. For example, *www.shattterdmen.com* is a support group for abused men. Dads_in_Family_Court (*http://groups.yahoo.com/group/DadsinFamilyCourt*) provides information for fathers who need help in family court *pro se* cases. We prefer to help those services by sending people their way when they need help, instead of starting new services that do the same thing. Where such services do not exist, we work with other organizations to bring awareness of the lack of resources and to enable the placement of those services. In Topeka, Kansas, we are now working with the Kansas Chapter of the National Congress for Fathers and Children or NCFC and other groups towards creating the Topeka Men's Resource Center."

The statistics concerning Men with health issues—diabetes, heart disease and prostate cancer are staggering. If Men who are Fathers are not healthy, they cannot adequately nurture and mentor their children and succeed in moving their families forward. What programs will the Million Dads March put in place to address the critical issue of Men's Health?

"Again, instead of starting our own programs to deal with men's health, we prefer to work with those organizations that are already working to bring equality between men's and women's health," Mr. Lessman responded. "Men's health is a major issue that has long been ignored. Women's health spending vastly outsources men's health spending. Consequently women outlive men by several years. Spending on such women's health concerns as breast cancer receive five or ten times the funding as men's health concerns such as prostate cancer, despite the similar infection and death rates.

I noted that the Million Dads March has succeeded in providing Men who are Fathers with an opportunity to demonstrate that they care very deeply about their children and families. When I asked Mr. Lessman to talk about the legacy of the Million Dads March he offered the following:

"Questions about legacy seem to indicate times past. At the Million Dads March, we won't quit until our goals are reached and there really is equality between men and women. We learned important lessons from our first year. These lessons will and are being studied. We are learning from the past and working towards a better and brighter future for every man, woman, and child on earth. Those who want to be part of the solution are encouraged to contact us and work with us."

ALVIN F. POUSSAINT, M.D.

"... A CHILD'S SELF-ESTEEM COMES FROM
MASTERING THEIR ENVIRONMENT.
MOTIVATING A CHILD SHOULD BE
A LIFE-LONG PROCESS ..."

ALVIN F. POUSSAINT, M.D., is a father; a husband; an author of a myriad of books and articles; an expert on children, race relations in America, diversity, and the dynamics of prejudice whose views are constantly sought out by the media; a consultant to government agencies and private corporations; a Professor of Psychiatry and the Faculty Associate Dean of the Harvard Medical School; the Director of the Media Center at the Judge Baker Children's Center; a member of the Academy of Child & Adolescent Psychiatry; and a Fellow of the American Association for the Advancement of Science. Although the world "beats a path to his door," hangs on his every word, and showers him with accolades and honors, in the eyes of his daughter and son, Dr. Poussaint is just simply "Dad." Amazingly, the center of Dr. Poussaint's universe lies squarely with his family.

So, how is Dr. Poussaint able to balance "being all things to all people" with his role as a Father? He says it's all about being disciplined and making time for your children.

"Well," Dr. Poussaint explained, "I think you schedule your life in such a way that you are able to play a dominant role in the lives of your children, but you are always stretched and you are always juggling. I have to make special efforts to spend time with my children. For instance, with my young daughter—I can't work late at night even if I wanted to. I keep my travel out of town to a minimum. When I do travel, I keep it to one night away from home so that I can spend as much time with her as possible. I see her in the mornings—before I leave for work—at breakfast. I see her in the evenings at dinner. And if my wife and I need to go away on extended business trips, we take her with us if we can. There are a lot of errands that I have to do and I take her along. For instance, when I go shopping, I take her with me. That helps keep a lot of contact going between her and me. You have to be disciplined about your time and you have to make time for your kids."

I was curious about the role models that Dr. Poussaint might have had as he made the transition from childhood to manhood.

"I had a big family—I had four older brothers and two older sisters and one younger sister. They all influenced me, but they were not immediate role models in the sense of 'who did I want to be like.' That mostly came from school teachers. There were women teachers in elementary school who were very supportive of me. Also, when I was nine years old I was sick with rheumatic fever and spent six months in a convalescent home. I got the idea of being a doctor from the doctors and nurses I came into contact with during that time. I was ten years old when I came out of the hospital and I had made up my mind I wanted to be a doctor. Those doctors— white doctors—who were there at the hospital were the role models. In junior high, I played the clarinet and had a music teacher who was very supportive. In junior high and in high school, I had my eye on a goal, so my role models were secondary. I looked for people who would be supportive and encouraging, but I knew what my mission was."

Was Dr. Poussaint given any advice about the duties and responsibilities of Fatherhood? And what advice was he given about selecting a mate who would eventually become the parent of his children?

"No, I don't remember getting any advice about becoming a Father," he responded. "Yet I learned about the duties and responsibilities of Fatherhood on my own. When my son was born, I was reading material about Fatherhood and I had an idea as to what kind of Father I wanted to be. I knew I didn't want to be like my father. I felt that he was too remote. There was not a lot of interaction. Occasionally, we did do some things with him but he wasn't the kind of dad who took you out to the movies and things like that. My mother did those types of things. As far as advice about selecting a mate—I was told to marry someone who I liked— someone whom I felt was going to be a good and kind mother.

That's not always easy to figure out, especially if the person doesn't already have a child yet. There is a dramatic change in husbands and wives when they have a child. You see parts of them that you've never seen before. A case that comes to mind is that of a very bubbly young woman who wanted very much to have a child. She became pregnant and after the child was born she suffered a very severe case of post partum depression. There was a dramatic change in this woman's personality as a result of having a child. There are bodily and psychological changes that occur in women giving birth. Some women don't know that they are going to get panicked about breastfeeding. Once you become a parent, you look to becoming more like your parents. You can't always predict what your mate is going to be. Look for someone who is kind and nurturing."

And what advice about parenting and the selection of a mate does Dr. Poussaint plan to pass on to his own children?

"Well, with my son, I think he has a good idea from me what kind of father he wants to be. We interact a lot. When we see each other, he greets me and kisses me on the cheek. We talk about his work, his school, his girlfriend. We always stay in touch regularly—even through college. And he—I know—likes the relationship. As I see him relate to his little sister, he is warm and nurturing. I tell him that he has to be involved and caring with his child in every way. Since he's a modern kid, he doesn't have those lines drawn between the roles of father and mother. He's not going to be some old-style dad. I haven't talked to him about choosing a mate. He will probably try to select someone who's a good mother. You can't always tell whether someone will be a good parent. But, it's certainly something that people should think and talk about," Dr. Poussaint responded.

Dr. Poussaint recommends "sticking with your kids and supporting and aiding their development; being patient with them while constantly keeping in mind the opportunities to teach them, to help them grow, and help them achieve a sense of mastery."

"Let them have some independence in making their own choices. Being patient with them as they get older is a challenge and it can be difficult not imposing your own will or ideas too strongly on them. I don't believe in corporal punishment. With younger kids, discipline is not an issue. You can say 'No' to something that they're doing. If it is something dangerous—such as the child picking up a knife—you can just simply tell them to put the knife down, not to pick it up, and then you take the knife away. With discipline at the age of two years old, you're simply teaching them about the world. For instance, if a child is eating and then decides to push his or her plate off the table and it falls onto the floor, the child may be attempting to find out what happens when he or she pushes the plate off the table. They are experiencing the world and they are learning. One of the challenges of parenting is being patient," he explains. "With a two year old who is pushing the limits, parents have to clarify the boundaries. Parents should tell a two year old that he shouldn't push the plate off the table and indicate from their tone that they expect him to learn self-control. But parents must still be patient and not lose their own self-control by yelling, etc."

So, what are the joys—the rewarding aspects of parenting?

"The joys of watching your child developing . . . speaking and talking—the positive feedback, love and mutuality. Very often, they are a lot of fun," he says warmly. "You get a joy out of teaching them things and watching them learn the things that you've taught them."

Our conversation moved to the issue of adequate resources and support services for Men who are Fathers. Are there adequate resources and support services for Men who are Fathers?

"No," Dr. Poussaint said flatly. "I don't think there are enough resources and support services for Men who are Fathers. Most resources and support services function for and are centered around women. You need places where men feel comfortable—like the Boys & Girls Club, Big Brothers, or the YMCA—and where they can ask questions. Men are not as likely to go to a pediatrician. Men should be encouraged to go to the pediatrician along with the mothers of their children. Parenting education at school is needed. Fathers should be included in the parenting education mothers get."

And, in Dr. Poussaint's view, what are the greatest challenges faced by our young males? What are the most critical issues that they must resolve?

"For young males the greatest challenge in making it into manhood is the issue of their social economic background. In the African American community, we have one million young males who are incarcerated. One of the greatest challenges for our young males is learning to navigate the system without getting trapped into something that is going to be damaging to them, like jail, substance abuse and crime. There are a lot of traps out there. They need people—role models—who are committed to keeping them on the right track and who are also helping to support their achievements through education—and sports, too. There needs to be more of a male environment and more male resources in the community."

So, what should we tell our young males about the duties and responsibilities and issues related to Fatherhood that we are not telling them?

According to Dr. Poussaint, it all comes down to being an involved father. "We should be telling our young males to be involved fathers; basically, being an involved father is what it comes down to. I say that because there are some young Black males who are fathers of a child who lives down the street from them and they don't see the child. And that's because they don't know that they have a role—a critical role—in that child's life. They don't know that fathers are important. And there are numerous studies which show that where fathers are involved in their children's lives, these children do better in school and are less likely to commit crimes."

How should we convey to our children the importance of having or developing a sense of direction in their lives?

"I think all along you are helping or should be helping to give direction to your children. From pre-school to high school, you're teaching them how to cope, solve problems, adapt to the environment, and negotiate problems that develop in their lives. You have to be ready to be flexible as children change to allow them to grow. When a child becomes an adolescent, you can't treat him like an eight-year old. You have to grow with them and allow them to make choices—even when the choices are not good choices—so they can learn how to become competent adults."

What should we teach our children about motivation? How do we teach them to become self-motivated? When should we begin this process?

"Well, I think one of the ways to motivate a child is to compliment them early on when they accomplish something—whether it's stacking blocks or drawing a picture. Show appreciation for the things that they do on their own. A child's self-esteem comes from mastering their environment. Motivating a child should be a life-long process. When they make an effort to do something, you stay on the positive side. When they have problems, you could say, 'Let's work on it together.' Or you could have them work on the problem themselves and then come to you when they feel they have a plan. For example, when my son had problems or needed help with his homework, I'd ask him to work out the problems and then show it to me and I would tell him what I thought. I would not do his homework for him."

MARTIN G. RAMEY

"... MANHOOD AND FATHERHOOD ARE LINKED TOGETHER ..."

He is the creator of a syndicated column, The Manhood Line, that deals with topical male-oriented issues. MARTIN G. RAMEY is also a licensed and ordained minister, state certified probation officer, state certified substitute teacher for Grades 6 through 12 and an award-winning broadcast and print journalist who resides in Indianapolis, Indiana. And when I sat down to talk with Mr. Ramey about issues directly and indirectly related to Fatherhood, he had no problem sharing his views.

I asked Mr. Ramey if he had received any advice about Fatherhood. What was he told about Fatherhood? Who told him?

"I'd like to thank you for this interview, because there are a few things I'd like your readers to know about this matter of fatherhood. Manhood and fatherhood are forever linked together. If a man is a quality man, a man of character, when his lovely bride comes up to him and says the 'phrase that pays' ('I'm pregnant'), he had it already in him to be a good father. Like many men who grew up in the sixties, I am a card-carrying member of 'The Old School.' I have to credit my own father with his wisdom about manhood and fatherhood, both verbal and non-verbal. My dad wasn't much of a 'talker,' but more of a 'doer.' He worked in a factory much of his life, which instilled the work ethic in me at an early age. He also was one who didn't take much in the way of 'back talk' from myself or my sister. I knew that he was proud of many of my accomplishments, and he still loved me in spite of my 'cutting up' every once in a while. But, like most men who came through segregation into the Civil Rights era and after, he believed in providing for his family. To him, fatherhood was raising your children to learn how to support home and family, as well as having a desire to work and provide for a family, with lots of love thrown in. Also to him, manhood involved matching his walk with his talk. No earthly father was, and is perfect, but my Dad did manage to teach me that the best part of fatherhood was raising your kids to uplift a good family name in the community," Mr. Ramey responded.

The conversation turned to selecting a mate. I wanted to know if Mr. Ramey received any advice and if so, what was he told and who told him.

"The best advice on seeking a wife also came from my Dad. It wasn't so much a 'list' of the ideal qualities, but he did tell me that a man has to be careful. Once the wedding bands go on, women who would not give you the time of day when you were single, would do their level best to try to bed you once you got married. My dad also gave me the following advice: 'Never where you work, and never where you live!' Translated, this means that once you are married, slipping around and adultery were forbidden. The one you got was the one you stayed with. My mother and father were married for about 30 years before he died. His walk and his talk were one . . . because there were no other 'sistahs' sneaking around our home, or in his private life."

In Mr. Ramey's view, what are the challenges that Men who are Fathers must resolve in the Millennium?

"The chief thing that I find that Men need to do is to reassert who wears the pants in the home . . . and it ain't Mama, it's Daddy! The key challenge is to get back to the grass roots level of what worked in the past. If your child needs discipline, then Daddy, *you* take care of it. If the family goes to church, Dad needs to take them . . . and not just drop them off for someone else to educate in the ways of God. In short, Men have to realize that manhood and fatherhood are linked. If you are not a quality man, you won't be much of a father. Another thing that men and fathers are going to have to resolve is, to 'lighten the load' so to speak, in our homes, of those things that are going to be harmful to our wives and children. That means we can't sit around and watch cable sports all weekend, and wonder why we don't interact with our wives and children. Cut the cable. Get rid of the DSS. Stop 'stocking up' your home bar and your garage with the 'latest.' Your child is only going to be in Pampers for a few short years. Turn around, and they will be asking you for money for lunch. Turn around again, and they will be asking you for the keys to the car. Turn around again, and they will be heading off to start their own lives, with their own wives and husbands."

Does Mr. Ramey feel that there are adequate resources and support systems for Men who are Fathers?

"As long as a man has the skills to work, there will be support systems. The problem today is that there are not enough men who are WILLING to talk with one another about manhood and fatherhood who are average, run-of-the-mill, hard-working men. We have been bombarded with so many 'famous' fathers and 'infamous' children and wives that we have forgotten that fathers talked to each other, and with each other. There was a time not that long ago when there were no government grants or social programs. Older fathers—in a new father's family—would pull him aside and 'school' him on fatherhood. They would also be available if the brother had questions. This doesn't happen as much as it should today. WE have been conditioned to think that our jobs mean more than our families, in our modern era. One last thing: There MUST be communication between men of all races concerning manhood and fatherhood. Right now, men are STILL fragmented because of race and class. Until men love each other for who they are, and can see beyond the color and class issue, we are not going to be that effective in this new millennium."

When asked to identify resources and support systems that he would like to see put in place for Men who are Fathers that he believes do not already exist, Ramey had this to say:

"Here are four, right off the bat. One, the politicians need to *kill* the Marriage Tax. If this were to happen, *overnight* marriage would regain its luster over 'living together.' Two, *single* fathers ought to *marry* the mother of their children, instead of being encouraged by society to 'breed more bastards' so that the state can take care of them with my tax money. Three, make premarital counseling mandatory before giving a couple a marriage license. Four, provide extra tax incentives for wives to stay home instead of heading off to work, if they are married. Work and providing are a man's job.

I noted that Mr. Ramey is a non-custodial father and asked him to share with us the challenges and issues that he had to resolve. I wanted to know if he had any advice to offer other non-custodial fathers.

"As I mentioned earlier, manhood and fatherhood are linked together. There are times that a man is going to fail in marriage. The key thing that I have had to remember, thanks to a great network of the brotherhood, and quality women, is that just because you have failed, does not mean you are a failure. It means that you are human. Even as a Christian. And, as a Christian, I have to keep in mind the biblical truth about failures: One cannot be bitter, one cannot seek to 'get even,' and one cannot 'blame' the children for a marriage break up. 'Be not conformed to this world, but be ye transformed by the renewing of your mind—Romans 12:1 King James Version'—which I have shortened for the sake of space. The best advice I can give men who are non-custodial fathers is the following: Your children, eventually, will get up in years and come to seek you out. Be ready to tell them that the end of the marriage was *not* their fault and that you will, and still, love them. This piece of advice I got from my pastor, Reverend Dr. Fitzhugh L. Lyons, Sr. who has been preaching the gospel for more than 50 years and has seen what God can do to restore broken family relationships. Another piece of advice—pay your child support the best that you are able, and *demand* that the courts and politicians *enforce* visitation rights as aggressively as they do child support payments. Judges listen to those who carry voter registration cards. So do those who warm the seats on Capitol Hill. Another piece of advice—build a legacy for your children. I have the columns that I write, and other material I have been 'setting aside,' including letters, for a record of who I am and what I stand for. My oldest son has received his 'packet' and my two other children have these 'legacy packets' waiting for them from me. Lastly, if you are a Christian, *pray* for your children. Pray that they meet good people. Pray that God will send them a mate that is a quality person, a helper instead of a hindrance. Pray that publications, such as **IN SEARCH OF FATHERHOOD® Forum For and About the Fathers of the World**, will be around to spread the truth about fathers, instead of the mainstream press. You can pray for them every day and not have to worry about how they are doing. God is already on the case."

When Mr. Ramey was asked to discuss the advice or key pieces of information that Men who are Fathers should pass on to their children about parenting, selecting a mate, and male-female relationships, he offered the following:

"Let's take the last one first. If she can out-drink you, out-cuss you, and out-fight you, Son, she is not a lady, but a longshoreman. She is *not* a woman whom I would give my blessing for you to get married to. The important thing is—if a young woman won't act like a lady, nor want you as 'her man' to treat her like a lady, then you don't need to be involved with her. As far as selecting a mate . . . if *you* are a Christian, *she* needs to be a Christian. There are already far too many marriages between men and women who are *not* going in the same direction. If you *both* are not going in the same direction, one of you can't carry the both of you, regardless of how good she looks, or how much money he has in his pocket. Brothers, I'm going to make it plain. W*hen* you select a mate, make sure she takes *your* name. *No Hyphens!* If she won't take your name, to love, honor, and obey, then *stay away!* I'm in my second marriage. Both of the women I have been married to have my name. My ex-wife was a lot of things, but she still carries my name. And *she* claims to be a feminist. And I might as well throw some more gasoline on the fire. Brothers, don't bed her until you *wed* her. I don't care how good she looks, or how much 'sweet talk' she wants to throw your way, or how much she wants to 'challenge' your manhood. If a woman says you are *less* than a man for *not* sleeping with her, then *move on!* As far as parenting . . . *Relax.* Parents are *going* to make mistakes. However, don't forget to discipline with love and *be consistent.* Plus, if you treat the mother right, the child will follow. And, remember to not turn your kids out to be carbon copies of *you.* Let them find out who they are, and encourage them to follow their dreams, while reminding them that the Bible is *not* their enemy, but is their friend. A parent's main job is to raise someone else's husband or wife (your son or daughter). If you have any consideration for their future spouse, *don't* load your kid up with an unrealistic view of life. Teach them early how to pick the right friends and stay away from the wrong ones. Teach them the value of work. Teach them the value of saving. Teach them the value of church and tithing. You won't go wrong, and their future spouses will praise your name to the heavens."

And who were his role models as he made the journey from childhood to manhood?

"There are soooooooo many! Cartoons, music, books, historical figures, etc. I have built a firm sense of humor because I had a father who danced with life, rather than complain about it! However, my best role model came to me at the age of 28 when I accepted Jesus Christ as my Lord and Savior, and lived life through *his* eyes, instead of mine. The only reason why Christianity is dull is because the people are dull. God is *not* dull, nor is the Bible. It's never too late for a man to be a good man, or a great father. It's a matter of making choices and sticking with them. A man can always gather more wisdom. As an 'Old Schooler,' I can remember what it *used* to be like in the home. My Dad was also a great role model, but God is a much better one at this time in my life. Plus, I wasn't 'raised' in the 'church'. This is a major-league revelation for someone. Being in church does not mean that one has a right relationship with God through Jesus Christ. It doesn't take a village to raise a child. It takes a mom and a dad," says Ramey.

And what about men's health issues? Is there an adequate focus on them? Mr. Ramey says "No!"

"No, I do not feel that there has been an adequate focus on men's health issues, because the feminized mainstream press wants to see women remain healthy and men remain sick, dead, or dying. Who works in the high-risk jobs? Men. Who fights the wars? Men. Then it would stand to reason that health care issues should involve men's health. WE are the ones who are carrying the lion's share of the load. If more women would stop trying to compete with men, they wouldn't have all these 'modern' ailments. It's interesting. The rise in the rate of breast cancer, ovarian cancer, and other cancers can be traced to three things—Abortion, Stress, and Alcohol. It's funny that our grandmothers didn't have to contend with heart disease, strokes, alcoholism, depression, etc. They took care of the home, the kids, and their husbands and lived to be ripe in age and wisdom. Now, you have female executives in their 40s who are stroking out on the job, or sucking up the booze bottle, or popping pills from Prozac to Zoloft, and having abortions. Now *you* tell me who really needs to get back to the home with the children. The men—who are supposed to be working—or the married career women who are trying to do the things that feminists told them that men should *not* be doing?"

Thirty, forty and even fifty years ago, there was virtually no discussion of men's issues—at least not publicly—or the need of resources and support services for Men who are Fathers. I asked Mr. Ramey to describe for us what he believes has happened or is happening in our society that is resulting in a loud outcry from Men who are Fathers for support services and resources.

"Men don't want new groups. Men just want things to be fair. If society demands that men be loving towards their kids, but don't encourage women to be loving towards the same kids, then society needs to take a good look in the mirror. T.D. Jakes said it best in one of his books: 'A nation of women can't raise up a nation of men!' Call me a sexist if you want to, but it is the *man's* job to win the bread, and the *woman's* job to shape the home. If the equation is out of sync, the home will be a mess. We are living in an era where rights have been taken away from men, step by step, by people who write laws who can't even run their own households. How many men 'pushed' through 'tougher' child support payment laws, *then* went through a divorce and demanded that they be 'exempt' because of political affiliation? More than you would want to know—and I am a person who has worked in the media and seen it happen. We are living in a modern era which I can best describe as 'The Era of the 70/30 Split'—meaning every adulterer, murderer and stalker gets to 'set the tone' for the social agenda because of their 'allegedly' being in a 'better' lifestyle than the rest of us. They are the 30 percent. What poppycock! Meanwhile, the 70 percent . . . the rest of us . . . have to put up with this kind of madness as being 'normal'. Perfect example. I had a meeting with a woman who was having disciplinary problems with her pre-teenage son. She's a single mother and has other kids besides this one. She asked me what she should do? I asked her: 'What size shoe do you wear?' She said: 'A size six.' I told her: 'Then, sister, you need to put that size six up your child's backside until he realizes that what Mama says—*goes!*' This is *not* child abuse . . . but child preservation. If that woman would use her size six, a police officer would *not* have to use his *nine* (Police Department issue pistol) to control the boy when he hits sixteen and won't listen to anyone," Ramey responded.

So, are we adequately equipping our young males with the tools that they will need to become successful adults—professionally and personally? Whose responsibility is it to equip our young males with the tools that they need to become successful adults—should the responsibility be shared jointly by parents, schools and churches in the community within which our young males live? Or should this responsibility be solely shouldered by the parents?

"I know that the tools and resources are out there for our young men to achieve," Ramey remarked. "But many of them have made the choice to dig their own hole with the shovel of crime and the 'easy Rap life.' Now, many of them have prison records and are behind the eight ball because a man with a prison number is *not* going to get the good jobs needed to provide for his family. It rests with the home. Back in the day, the *last* type of parent you would want to be the child of was a *single* parent. *Those* parents had *guts*, and wouldn't take any lip from the kids. *now* you have a whole generation of parents—even single parents—who don't want to parent. If the home won't do, society can't do. Let me end this interview on an inspiring note. It is *not* too late for our young men and young women to turn around . . . even with a prison record. First, they have to accept responsibility for their own actions. Second, they have to get their education and work records rebuilt.

Third, they need to get off their butts, turn off the MTV and BET and get out and get a job and start at the bottom like the *rest* of us did. The young man who *wants* to advance in society and put his past behind him *can* do it if he *wants to!* Some of my young brothers need to marry 'their baby's mama' and help turn her into an honest woman. Some of my young brothers need to stop taking the easy way out with the crack pipe, the half pint, and the Rap video. Some of my young brothers need to stop playing games with God, with the church, and with society and learn that 'Success' only comes before 'Work' in the dictionary. Yes, I'm a little rough on the young brothers. But there were some older brothers who were rough with me. I turned out okay. They can, too . . . but a man can't be a punk and still call himself a man. You can't be a father if *you* are sitting on your blessed assurance and are forcing the mother of your children out to work, when *you* didn't marry her, and aren't looking for a job or to better your own education. I wear a size 13 shoe. Consider that myself, and other men in the community will keep on putting them in young men's butts until *they* realize that you can't call yourself a man or a father until *you* get out and get a job and provide for those kids that you birthed. Marry the mama, and end the drama. *Word!*"

Cognizant of the fact that he is one of the few syndicated columnists that focuses on men's issues on a regular basis, I asked Mr. Ramey why he writes about men's issues and what motivates him.

"America has allowed itself to be sold a bill of goods concerning manhood and fatherhood, especially among men of color. At first, no one cared if Black men in general, or Black fathers in particular, were 'slipping' in impact, respect, and authority in the home, workplace, and church. Now, manhood and fatherhood are attacked routinely, across the board as the anti-male fury has seeped into what I would call 'the feminized mainstream press.' Many of those who 'down' men seem to forget that if it wasn't for a man in the equation, they would *not* be here! I write on men's issues through *The Manhood Line* because there is a *need.* As a journalist, minister, and writer, I learned more than a few lessons along the way. In our 'high tech' age, we are missing a chance to pass those lessons on to the next generation like our fathers and grandfathers did with us. All I am doing is putting forth basic biblical, business, and common sense that is available to any man who wants it . . . or needs it. I'm truly blessed by the fact that although many men read *The Manhood Line*, there are many women who read the column on a regular basis as well . . . and they hear what I am saying . . . and agree with much of what I write. But I am going after *men*! It's the brothers who need to be told that *they* are worthwhile, and their contribution to society *does* matter. It's been said that 'It takes a village to raise a child'. Not in my book. All it takes is Mom—and *Dad*! And, until *both* parents are welcomed to the family table, you *won't* have a family. You'll just have a collection of individuals grabbing for what they can get, not focusing on what they can give. Let me wrap this up, because I can see some folks reaching for the No Doz and coffee. The hour *is* late. But, my wife, Adele, is my biggest cheerleader in my getting the column started way back in 1995. The Lord has blessed where the column is seen. Great and courageous editors such as yourself run my column. And, a strong widow by the name of Dr. Mary Tandy, publisher of *The Indiana Herald* gave me my 'shot' in being a columnist when no one else would. In fact, let me close with one of Dr. Tandy's favorite quotes: 'When a woman disrespects a man, she is actually slapping the face of *his mother*.' You can't get more real . . . than that!"

ALMAS JAMIL SAMI'

MAINTAINING FATHERHOOD STATUS

Damn! I can't believe I lost all of my stuff in storage. "I'm sorry, but we had to sell your things to recoup our losses, sir." I wanted to punch him. Hard. But I realized that it was not his fault because I did not pay the storage bill. It was solely mine. The proverbial buck stopped with me. I was the one who let my family down . . . again.

I had placed practically all of our possessions in storage three months prior when we had been evicted. Now we stayed in an abandoned duplex that a friend of a friend let us use until I could somehow get my groove back. My wife was eight months pregnant and I was just recovering from a back and knee ailment. But what really and truly ailed me was my mind. I had lost the ability to "think" my way through life. I had lost my rhythm and could not find the essence of who I was. Lost my fight. Lost myself somewhere in a maze of professional failures and disappointments. I was mentally, spiritually and physically crippled and fell behind on the payments and as a consequence, the storage company cut the lock on the door and sold, piece by piece, all of our belongings. I didn't think about my things. I could only think about my wife and children. How will I tell my son and daughter that they had lost all of their toys, books, clothes, music tapes and video games? Everything! It was the final humiliation for them in a summer of humiliation. Their friends had seen us pack up and leave. I wondered if they actually knew that my children were going to be homeless. What did they tell their school buddies where we were moving to? How embarrassing that must have been for them. And now, I had to somehow tell them that just about all that they held near and dear was lost forever.

"I got some bad news for y'all." I saw the look on their faces as I recounted for them what I had learned earlier that day. They were sad. Real sad. They looked like they should have looked after just learning that they were not only homeless, but their father had messed up again. Their father's failures had once again altered their perception of reality. What horrific event would befall them next? How would they recover? I could hardly hold my head up. I wanted to leave the family. I fully understood why so many men find their way to the door of no return. The urge to leave is so very, very strong. I knew that my wife could get on welfare and really do much better without me . . . at least financially. However, one single idea or notion ensured that I maintained my sanity. One solitary bit of truth made the difference. The difference between being a man and being an understanding man. The difference was that I was a father. I was a daddy. In spite of all that I had lost, I had somehow maintained the status of being a daddy. Truly God's blessing!

I knew that my children knew me as a father first. Not a failure. Not a loser. But rather a father. A man who had been there for them. They knew that everything hinged on me. And since I had been there to fend off uncaring teachers, or disrespectful store managers, or unfriendly neighbors, they saw me as "Dad." They saw me as a man who loved them and made sure that they always knew it. They might have had other concerns about life given all that we had been through, but they knew in the deepest recesses of their souls that they had a daddy who loved them and was proud of them. They had come to know me as a consistent force in their lives. I was simply always there. They had seen me rip into teachers on their behalf more than once. No one messed with them. They knew that no matter what they were facing, they would face it with their dad and mama. Even if I was away or out of town, they knew that I would drop everything and attend to their needs if they called on me. I wasn't the greatest provider. But what I did give them does not have a price. I gave them ME! Always ME!

I wanted to cry tears of joy when I learned they were more concerned about me and their mama's stuff than they were about the toys and other items that were lost in storage. Oh, they were not happy to lose their belongings, but they kept their priorities straight. They had seen our example and were now following it. They knew that my blood was running through their veins and that we were a family. My spirit would always be with them. They remembered the lectures. (The ones that I thought were never really heard.) They remembered that their mama and daddy loved them. Somehow, through the graces of God, I was able to become their friend. No, I don't mean that they could disrespect me. I did not set out to become one of them, but I did want them to have a father who was "friendly" to them. When you think about it, that is one of the missing ingredients that leaves our children vulnerable to gangs and other predators. Of course, there are other factors such as failure to maintain a loving household. Or "consistently" being there for them and a myriad of other parental shortcomings. However, lost in all of this is the fact that gang members offer "friendship" to people who have never had intimate "family-friends" who they bonded with or truly built trust around. Human trust.

When a child is born, he or she looks to mama and daddy as their "Gods on earth." We are their providers of not only the tangible necessities in life like food and shelter, but also love, honor, trust, discipline, encouragement, and guidance to name only a few. Children remain trustful until we drop the ball. We drop havoc into their lives when they can no longer look to mama or daddy as the proverbial "Rocks of Gibraltar." Rocks of friendship. Rocks of trust. Rocks of comfort. Rocks of understanding. Rocks of patience. Rocks of wisdom. Rocks of love. When these structures or "Rocks" are missing, then gangs are sure to move in and fill voids.

I remember talking to my son one evening after work when he said, "Gangs aren't that bad, dad." I probed further to try and get a handle of where he was coming from. "I met some brothers who were in a gang today at the park playing basketball. We laughed and played around. I think I have some new friends. They even let me play in games with them!" I studied him as he burst with what could only be termed as raw excitement. He beamed as if he had just gotten off of a roller coaster. After a while I told him that they were "recruiting" him or looking for others like themselves who came from "child-unfriendly" homes. If my son hadn't already bonded with me, then he would have bonded with the other unfortunate gang members over a period of time . . . depending on how chaotic or unfriendly his home was at the time.

This bond or friendship with children can be maintained over distances as well. If you have a loving bond with your children, they will follow you off of any cliff with a smile on their faces. Sure they want all of the "stuff" that comes from the store. But if I had a dollar for every "stuff-rich" kid who was miserable, I'd be a wealthy man. They have a TV in their room, VCR, video games, boxes and boxes of toys and all of the latest styles of clothes in the closet. Yet they are every bit as lost and lonely as their parents who attempt to buy what only time and love could give . . . caring parents. I KNOW for a fact that children value your love, friendship and time much more than anything that can be bought at any store. And yes, they can get that from long distances too. It would be ideal if you were in their presence everyday, but your love and attentiveness can be felt (and appreciated) over long distances and even years. If they KNOW you; I mean really KNOW you, then they will cherish the bond and grow to depend on your love, which will add stability to their lives. Always.

I have found that the quickest and surest way to get your children to trust you is to let them in your world. Let them in on your own fears and failures. How do YOU deal with your own pain and frustration? What would YOU do over again if you were their age? What were YOUR childhood dreams and aspirations? What makes YOU frightened? What was YOUR childhood like? Whom did YOU grow up with? Did any of the other kids in the neighborhood scare YOU? What was it like growing up where YOU grew up? What inspires YOU? What are YOUR dreams? Do YOU have a favorite uncle or aunt? WHO ARE YOU????

Let them into your world. They will surely let you in theirs. Then sit back and watch them grow and blossom into the positive, loving, caring young people that you always wanted them to be.

Give them yourself, and they will give you an uncommon love that will leave you feeling like you can hold your head up no matter what you have or haven't done with YOUR life. They will show you the depths of human love. And you will again find that loving child in you that you only thought left many years ago. No, my friend, that child lives in the children that sprang from your loins. You are there. Look.

JOEP ZANDER

THE LABOUR PARTY AND FATHERS IN THE NETHERLANDS—NEGOTIATING BETWEEN THE WRINKLES IN THE LACE CURTAIN

OCCUPATION

On 20 November 2000—Children's Rights Day—some 30 fathers tried to occupy the headquarters of the 'Partij van de Arbeid' (PvdA—Dutch governing Labour Party) in Amsterdam. They wanted the Party to pay more attention to the significance of fathers in the well-being of children. They struck a blow for shared care and access to children for both men and women.

The action led to a series of negotiations at all levels of the Party. It also led to the Labour Party hosting an open conference with protest representatives and other interested parties contributing to new policies for the Labour Party manifesto. Here is a short review and probing analysis of these events.

PvDA

The PvdA has always been rooted in the working classes, a tradition upheld by our present Prime Minister. The Party is founded on a number of socialist ideas, somewhat diluted of late. But in the last few decades feminism has given the party an important secondary ideological base. This variety of feminism, as others elsewhere, has covered itself in ambiguity with regard to the position of fathers. Theoretically, there is a desire for more paternal involvement in families. In practice, the intent is to accept fathers on mothers' terms alone and otherwise exclude them.

Unfortunately, political involvement in fatherhood issues has until now been found almost exclusively on the right of the political spectrum. All the more reason to carry out our action at the PvdA headquarters. The physical occupation didn't quite come off, it is true, but for a whole morning long, the main entrance to the party offices was thoroughly blocked.

DEVELOPMENTS

During the protest, there where negotiations with Party managers and members of parliament. Family policy is normally a subject left to the particular attention of the Labour women's group, who were thus closely engaged with the discussions.

Central to the negotiations was the Langeac Declaration (*see October 2001 issue* of **IN SEARCH OF FATHERHOOD® FORUM FOR AND ABOUT THE FATHERS OF THE WORLD**), which served as a key point of departure in our discussions. It was agreed that we should strive to raise these issues with the government and have a conference on this subject in tight liaison with the Party's National Executive, drawing attention to our deliberations both in the Party's own press outlets and if possible in wider related media. There was also a promise to let the banners hang for another week on the front of the building.

Two of the four members of our own organizational committee found this insufficient reason to stop our blockade. However, the majority of the 30 participants in the blockade thought it best to give the Labour Party the benefit of the doubt. Although a large number of journalists attended, there was little coverage of the action on the day itself. But later developments were well covered. Noteworthy was a television discussion programme involving young people where we received overwhelming support from both girls and boys.

NEGOTIATIONS

Mainly through lack of courage and full understanding on the part of members of parliament there were few tangible results from the promised discussions with the government, for example, on the question of PAS (Parental Alienation Syndrome). The Labour Party representatives however gained a far greater insight into the problems. The engagement and good will of the female head of the Party administration led to the PvdA women's group becoming the co-organizers of the conference. On 31 May 2001, the conference was held with the full backing of the National Executive Council of the Party. In the invitation to attend the conference, the following ground-breaking sentences were seen:

"On the one side there is a growing appeal from society to men to take up more caring tasks, on the other hand they are, in divorce cases, not seen as a responsible caring parent. The present practice of family law is oppressive to many of them, especially in those cases where they end up losing one parent (mostly their father) permanently, with all the traumatic results that ensue. It is remarkable that in the case of divorce there seems to be a relapse into traditional ideas on the division of care and work. Mothers seem to see themselves and are being seen as primary caretakers and refuse to distance themselves from their 'care capital'."

These remarkable sentences have until now probably never been heard from a mainstream women's organization. The results of negotiation within the oversight committee which had been set up were also interesting. There was an attempt to place the conference in the above context of apparently conflicted duality of fathers' and mothers' rights in families with new linkages drawn between the lack of real fathers' rights in relation to their children, social repression and malpractice in the shape of discrimination against fathers. In Holland, this incontestable dissipation of male rights has been witnessed while the actual caring responsibilities of fathers have continued to expand. The workshop dedicated to this matter was poorly attended due to the attraction exercised by the more technical workshops on judicial issues and PAS. We had expected some Labour Party and Labour women's group members to attend this particular workshop, but the workshop was marked by their absence. Moreover, Party officials did not succeed in mobilizing their own backbenchers. Thus, because we, the conference taskforce, decided to avoid over-attendance of one group of participants (fathers), the conference as a whole was also poorly attended.

THEORY AND PRACTICE

In the course of the lead-up to the conference we had noted on several occasions that what we were negotiating stood a chance of meeting strong resistance in practice. Nevertheless, Labour Party officials had difficulty in conceiving this. We tried to show what we meant by comparing our present situation in Holland with recent experience in New Zealand. A Shared Parenting Bill, allowing for a default of equal division of parental responsibility, was placed before Parliament in May 2000. However, the governing New Zealand Labour Party and women's organizations combined forces in an effort to stop the bill dead in its tracks.

It was assumed that in Holland our approach would be more mature. But the truth was that things were not much better. One female member of Parliament involved in the negotiations repeatedly brought up women's interests in order to oppose certain proposals. A male colleague of hers gave a prime example of political impotence. He actually advanced the notion that "it is an illusion to believe in the primacy of politics," a somewhat unusual position for a left-wing party to take.

However, we did manage to launch a discussion on the reasons for the equally feeble stance of male politicians in regard to anti-father discrimination and denial of paternal contact rights. In truth, it is regarded as a minus point when building up your status as a male politician to discuss or bring in personal problems. It did not surprise me in the least that in this arena, the original plan for the conference in the parliament building was less than a resounding success. The strategic situation is well illustrated by the upset that occurred when the first version of the invitation to attend was issued. In this invitation, pro-female activists were already seeking to bring in the position of women by demanding the inclusion of commentaries to the effect that, at the very least, such solutions to contact problems would reduce the amount of male violence against women.

WOMEN'S MOVEMENT

During the conference we determined that the failed workshop on the subject of childcare by men would be followed up by a round-table conference within the Dutch Parliament chaired by Mariette Hamer MP. Mrs. Hamer is responsible for family affairs in her party parliamentary delegation and was a member of the Party Commission that prepared the new election manifesto. In the preparation for this round-table conference the two people who had introduced the original workshop made the resultant text into a more comprehensive paper, strongly sustaining the theoretical points underpinning equal parenting. But, remarkably, the representative of the Women's Alliance for Reallocation of Care and Work, an organization financially supported by the government, refused to connect this to any practical legal consequences.

Instead, the Women's Alliance chose to personally attack the father who had prepared the original workshop by accusing him of retaining personal concepts signifying that women would have no interest in sharing the care of children. De facto, it is fair to say that he had concluded that women's self-interest does play into the present situation, but he also made clear that this showed a poor understanding of their own interests. This viewpoint is, in fact, paralleled by that of many female writers who claim similar ideas in well-established women's magazines (e.g., *Aminata Forna*). It seems that when bringing in ideas that are less than politically correct, the problem is compounded when their proponent is male.

The whole setup bears some comparison with the concept of the "lace curtain" as presented by Warren Farrell, Ph.D. The Women's Alliance was so angry that it refused to join the round-table conference with Mariette Hamer.

EQUAL PARENTING

The round-table conference was a success, in spite of the absence of the Women's Alliance. Our most important points regarding the redefinition of childcare responsibilities were positively received. Mrs. Hamer was more than willing to bring this matter to the attention of the Manifesto Committee. In fact, this initiative has led to the insertion of an interesting paragraph in the manifesto promising to implement equal care for both parents into law.

It was very surprising that in the first draft this paragraph was somehow left out of the concept text. The same happened to a positive commentary submitted by the Board of the Party, containing an amendment intended to secure unrestricted contact between parents and children.

It seems that some networking was taking place with people at higher levels in the party with a view to blocking such developments. We asked ourselves (and those who might know amongst our interlocutors) the source of such obstruction, and came to the conclusion that important male figures in the party were heavily influential in support of the "women's movement."

At the Party Congress in December 2001, both texts (the recovered original plus subsequent amendments) were incorporated into the election manifesto with the proviso that the word "unrestricted" was dropped for unknown and undiscussed reasons. In the meantime, an important and highly relevant article by Professor Hoefnagels, to be published in the Party's own magazine, was coming under heavy fire. In this context, it is crucial to appreciate the stabilizing influence of the taskforce we had helped to form. This comprised both user groups and politicians, with two administrative and one National Executive member of the

Party as well as two members of Parliament, who pursued their task with zest and competence.

THE "POLDERMODEL"

The Dutch fathers' movement has certainly registered some successes and made good use of the possibilities of the Dutch so-called "Polder model." The advantage of this model is the emphasis it places on talking and negotiating conflicting interests and viewpoints. The disadvantage is the resistance to change it engenders due to the way it encourages evasion of conflicting situations and decisions. It is very hard to set limits on our social and political behavior. Such policies, aimed at deterring us from anti-social behavior, have led to a number of unfortunate events in recent Dutch social experience.

Moreover, such attitudes give an opportunity to disregard judges' decisions and more than this to an actual disregard of the law by the judges themselves. For those not familiar with Dutch legal practice, it appears quite incredible that in Holland it is normal practice for lawyers or public prosecutors to combine these roles with that of judge. The business of family law thrives on voluntary interpretation of such legal concepts as "the best interest of the child" and this has led to a sense of chaos and confusion at the present time in Holland. The bald fact is that the concept of the child's best interests thus becomes so arbitrary and fickle that often, under such discretionary largesse, the interests become the opposite—those of the professionals practicing in this field.

FATHERING

The Dutch fathers' movement not only tries to get the politicians to listen but also to act and to set limits to attacks on the father-child relationship. There are now increasingly vocal objections to policies that blur the line between tolerable and intolerable behavior, which can be seen as an extension of the notion of "smothering" (Warren Farrell, Ph.D.) on a macro level. However, as a mark of hope, the political maneuverings described above may just result in the establishment of some core notions on the idea of fathering and their insertion into family policy development. Slowly but steadily, our view of fathering is changing, with the development of a view of the father as a mixture of a good listener, talker, care giver and boundary setter for children.

The biggest Dutch political party—the Labour Party—is clearly disposed to listen, that much is shown by our recent experience. Full of expectation, we look towards a new alliance of mothers and fathers, fatherhood and motherhood, never denying the accomplishments of feminism (but not its ugly sister—female supremacy), while acknowledging the full value of fatherhood.

CONTRIBUTORS

STEPHEN BASKERVILLE, PH.D. is a prolific author of articles on fathers' rights and men's issues, a Political Science Professor at Howard University in Washington, D.C., President of the American Coalition for Fathers and Children and a Contributing Editor to the quarterly international male parenting journal IN SEARCH OF FATHERHOOD(R) FORUM FOR AND ABOUT THE FATHERS OF THE WORLD which is exclusively published and distributed by BSI International, Inc.

MUHAMMAD NASSER BEY is the publisher of the *AAA Credit Guide, The Guide to Import-Export in Global Africa*; and is a broker for international business deals in Africa. Mr. Bey, who will be launching a new website for entrepreneurs, is also a voiceover actor and Father and lives in Philadelphia.

RANDY L. COLLINS is an antiques and collectable dealer, a disability rights activist, poet and Contributing Editor to the quarterly international male parenting journal IN SEARCH OF FATHERHOOD(R) FORUM FOR AND ABOUT THE FATHERS OF THE WORLD which is exclusively published and distributed by BSI International, Inc. Mr. Collins resides in Fort Wayne, Indiana.

LEONARD DANTZLER is an information technology professional, a member of the Board of the Directors of a professional non-profit information technology organization—BDPA Philadelphia Information Technology Thought Leaders—and a Father. Mr. Dantzler resides in Philadelphia.

WARREN FARRELL, PH.D. is a resident of California, the author of a series of best-selling books on men's issues which include "*Father And Child Reunion: How To Bring The Dads We Need To The Children We Love*" and "*Why Men Are The Way They Are.*" Dr. Farrell was a candidate in the 7 October 2003 California Gubernatorial Recall Election and has taught psychology, women's studies, political science and sociology at Georgetown University, Rutgers University and Brooklyn College. He has also taught in the School of Medicine at the University of San Diego in California and is a Contributing Editor to the quarterly international male parenting journal IN SEARCH OF FATHERHOOD(R) FORUM FOR AND ABOUT THE FATHERS OF THE WORLD which is exclusively published and distributed by BSI International, Inc.

DALE J. FRAZA is a father and author of two novels that were published in 2003 who lives in Florida. Mr. Fraza has also been a Contributing Editor to the quarterly international male parenting journal IN SEARCH OF FATHERHOOD(R) FORUM FOR AND ABOUT THE FATHERS OF THE WORLD which is exclusively published and distributed by BSI International, Inc.

THOMAS R. GOLDEN, LCSW is an author, speaker, and psychotherapist whose groundbreaking book, *Swallowed By A Snake: The Gift Of The Masculine Side Of Healing*, is helping men and women effectively deal with grief. Mr. Golden's work has been featured in the *New York Times, Washington Post, and U.S. News and World Report.* Currently, he is helping to create a website—StandYourGround.Com (*www.StandYourGround.com*) which serves as a resource for Fathers. Mr. Golden is also a Contributing Editor to IN SEARCH OF FATHERHOOD(R) FORUM FOR AND ABOUT THE FATHERS OF THE WORLD, a quarterly international male parenting journal exclusively published and distributed by BSI International, Inc.

L.T. HENRY authored the first-in-a-series of Fatherhood book projects—IN SEARCH OF FATHERHOOD® which was published in April 1998 by BSI International, Inc. During his lifetime, Mr. Henry was a photojournalist, sales and motivation trainer and classically trained jazz musician who performed with The Philadelphia Orchestra and with popular singer and film and television actress Della Reese.

THOMAS HOERNER is the Executive Liaison for the Dallas, Texas chapter of Fathers for Equal Rights, Inc. and a custodial father of three. Mr. Hoerner's highly acclaimed book, *"The Ultimate Survival Guide For The Single Father,"* has earned him the dual titles of *"America's Guru On Single Parenting"* and the *"King Of Guy-Talk On Running A Household."*

GARY A. JOHNSON is an accomplished facilitator, motivational speaker, the principal of Gary A. Johnson Company—a consulting firm which specializes in management, harrassment prevention and facilitation— and the founder of several Internet web sites, most notably, *Black Men In America.com* and *Gary's Homework Help Page,* the latter of which has been recognized by USA Today Education and NBCi as one of the best homework help sites on the Internet. Mr. Johnson's twenty-five year work experience, prior to becoming an entrepreneur, includes an 18-year stint with the federal government in a variety of disciplines. He served three years at the White House and was assigned to the National Security Council staff where he worked for three Assistants to the President for National Security Affairs. Mr. Johnson resides in Maryland with his wife and two sons.

JAMES KENNEDY is a lyricist, music producer, principal of M1 Entertainment and Oyster Shell Publishing and a Father who resides in Philadelphia, Pennsylvania.

THOMAS LESSMAN is an Equal Parenting Rights advocate and Chairman of the Million Dads March which is headquartered in Topeka, Kansas who orchestrated worldwide demonstrations by Fathers on Father's Day—Sunday, 15 June 2003. Mr. Lessman is also the President of the Kansas Chapter of the National Coalition of Fathers and Children.

ALVIN F. POUSSAINT, M.D. is the Director of the Media Center of the Judge Baker Children's Center and Professor of Psychiatry and Faculty Associate Dean for Student Affairs at Harvard Medical School in Boston, Massachusetts.

MARTIN G. RAMEY is the creator of *The Manhood Line*, a column published on the Internet and syndicated by Brainstorm Communications that deals with topical male-oriented issues, an award-winning print journalist, licensed and ordained minister, state certified probation officer, state certified substitute teacher for Grades 6 through 12 and a Contributing Editor to **IN SEARCH OF FATHERHOOD® FORUM FOR AND ABOUT THE FATHERS OF THE WORLD**, a quarterly international male parenting journal exclusively published and distributed by BSI International, Inc.

ALMAS JAMIL SAMI' is the founder and principal of Sohaja Publishing Company, author, lecturer, father of three, grandfather of one, the host of a weekly television show—"Scribz," and a Contributing Editor to **IN SEARCH OF FATHERHOOD(R) FORUM FOR AND ABOUT THE FATHERS OF THE WORLD**, a quarterly international male parenting journal which is exclusively published and distributed by BSI International, Inc.

JOEP ZANDER is an artist, pedagogue and Father who resides in The Netherlands. He is also a Contributing Editor to **IN SEARCH OF FATHERHOOD(R) FORUM FOR AND ABOUT THE FATHERS OF THE WORLD**, a quarterly international male parenting journal that is exclusively published and distributed by BSI International, Inc. Mr. Zander's activism in the Fathers' Rights arena and his success in having his child custody/child visitation rights case heard by the European Court of Human Rights has resulted in his being viewed by many as a Champion of Fathers' Rights in Europe.

SUPPORT SERVICES FOR FATHERS

AUSTRALIA

Australian Information and Support Services for Men Pty Ltd.—
Unit 5a, 21 Stud Rd., Bayswater Vic 3153 Australia. Telephone:
011 03 9738 2478. Facsimile: 011 03 9878 4725. Its website
address is *www.aissm.com.au.* E-mail messages can be sent to
info@aissm.com.au.

Men's Rights Agency—Post Office Box 28, Waterford, Queensland,
4183, Australia. Telephone: 011 07 3805 5611. Facsimile: 011
07 3200 8769. Visit the organization's website at
www.mensrights.com.au. E-mail messages can be sent to
mra@ecn.net.au.

Michael Green, Q.C.—Mediator and counselor and author of
*Fathers After Divorce—Building A New Life And Becoming A Successful
Separated Parent.* A *strong advocate of "shared parenting,"* Green can
be reached by telephone or facsimile at 011 02 9519 7988 or by
e-mail at *magnews@bigpond.com.*

Stepfamily Australia, Inc.—P.O. Box 1162, Gawler, South Australia
5118. Telephone: 011 08 8822 7007. Its website address is
www.stepfamily.asn.au. E-mail messages can be sent to
sasa@stepfamily.asn.au.

CANADA

Ex-Fathers—Contact Lloyd Gorling at RR1, Williamstown,
Ontario, K0C 2J0 Canada. Telephone: 613-931-2104/Facsimile:

613-931-2104. The website address for Ex-Fathers is *http:// www.kalypso@glen-net.ca.*

Fathers Battling Injustice—Contact Dave Foster at 1500 Royal Fork Rd., Box 57507, Toronto, Ontario, Canada M9P 3B6. Mr. Foster can be reached at *dave@canadian.net.*

The Children's Voice—Contact Bill Flores, President of The Children's Voice, Post Office Box 61027, Maple Grove Post Office, Oakville, Ontario L6J 7P5 Canada. Telephone and Facsimile: 905-829-3639. E-mail: *kidshelp@ican.net.*

Victoria Men's Centre—Contact Ken Wiebe at 1967 Oak Bay Avenue, Victoria, British Columbia V82 1E3 Canada.

FRANCE

L'Enfant Et Son Droit (A Child and His Right)—12 rue Alphand, 75013 Paris, FRANCE. Telephone: 01 33 0 1 45 81 19 84. Visit their website address at *http://www.magic.fr/enfant-papa/welcome.htm*

SWITZERLAND

Health in Prisons Project—**World Health Organization**—Avenue Appia 20, 1211 Geneva 27, Switzerland. Telephone: 011 41 22 791 2111. Facsimile: 011 41 22 79 1311.

UNITED KINGDOM

Families Need Fathers—134 Curtain Road, London EC2A 3AR England. Telephone: 011 44 0207 613 5060). Visit their website address at *http://www.fnf.org.*

MK Family Rights Initiative—Visit its website at *www.MKfamilyhuman-rights.org.* Its e-mail address is MK.familyrights@ntlworld.com

The Cheltenham Group—Acts as an advocate of men's rights issues through publishing, research and lobbying. Visit its website at *www.c-g.org.uk*. Its e-mail address is *bpw@c-g.org.uk*.

UK Men's Movement—This organization campaigns and lobbies for the protection of equitable rights for men and publishes a quarterly publication that explores men's rights issues. Visit its website at *www.ukmm.org.uk*.

UNITED STATES

CALIFORNIA
The National Men's Resource Center™. Visit their website at *www.menstuff.org* or send an e-mail to *menstuff@aol.com*.

National Latino Fatherhood and Family Institute—5252 East Beverly Boulevard, Los Angeles, CA 90022. Contact Jerry Tello, Executive Director of National Latino Fatherhood and Family Institute at 323-728-7770 or via e-mail at *nlffi@nlffi.org*.

COLORADO
Focus on the Family—8605 Explorer Drive, Colorado Springs, CO 80995. Its website address is *www.family.org*.

La Pa's—Contact Randy Mergler, M.S. and Roger Coughlan, LCSW at La Pa's at Transformation of Fatherhood. Telephone: 970-495-4624. La Pa's e-mail address is *dads@lapas.org* and its website address is *www.lapas.org*.

DISTRICT OF COLUMBIA
Health In Prisons Project—Regional Offices for the Americas/Pan American Health Organizations—525 23rd Street, N.W., Washington, DC 20037. Telephone: 202-974-3000. Facsimile: 202-974-3663.

Men's Health Network—Post Office Box 75792, Washington, D.C. 20013. Telephone: 202-543-6461. Facsimile: 202-543-2727. The organization's website address is *http://www.menshealthnetwork.org.* Its e-mail address is *info@menshealthnetwork.org.*

FLORIDA

Commission on Marriage & Family Support—Contact Anne Carpenter, Administrative Assistant at the Commission on Marriage & Family Support (formerly, Florida's Commission on Responsible Fatherhood) at 111 North Gadsden Street, Suite 200, Tallahassee, Florida 32301 Telephone: 850 488-4952 x135. Facsimile: 850-921-9070.

GEORGIA

100 Black Men of America, Inc.—141 Auburn Avenue, Atlanta, GA 30303. Telephone: 404-688-5100. Toll Free Telephone: 800-593-3411. Facsimile: 404-688-1024. 100 Black Men of America, Inc.'s web site address is *www.100BlackMen.com.*

HAWAII

Akamai University—Located in Hawaii, Akamai University offers a comprehensive Men's Studies and Fatherhood curriculum. Inquiries concerning admission requirements can be obtained by contacting Douglass Capogrossi, Ph.D., President of Akamai University at 193 Kinoole Street, Hilo, Hawaii 96720 USA. Akamai University's United States and Canadian telephone numbers are 1-877-934-8793 while its international telephone number is 1-808-934-8793. Visit Akamai University's website at *www.akamaiuniversity.us.*

KANSAS

Million Dads March—Thomas Lessman serves as Chairman of the Million Dads March. Its web site address is *www.MillionDadsMarch.org.* The Million Dads March's mailing address is 4121 N.E. Brier Road, Topeka, KS 66616. Telephone: 785-230-4546. Facsimile: 775-665-9230. The e-mail address for the Million Dads March is chairman@milliondadsmarch.org.

The National Center for Fathering—10200 West 75th Street, Suite 367, Shawnee Mission, KS 66213. Telephone: 913-384-4661 or 800-593-3237. Its website address is *www.fathers.com*

MARYLAND

African American Male Leadership Institute—Richard A. Rowe serves as the Executive Director of the African American Male Leadership Institute ("AAMLI"). Correspondence can be sent to AAMLI at its mailing address of P.O. Box 32025, Baltimore, MD 21208 or via e-mail at *AAMLI51@aol.com*. AAMLI's telephone number is (410) 637-5564 and its facsimile number is (410) 602-8067.

American Prostate Society—7188 Ridge Road, Hanover, MD 21807. Telephone: 410-859-3735. Facsimile: 410-850-0818. Its e-mail address is *info@ameripros.org*.

Gary's Homework Help Page—An award-winning homework help web site created by entrepreneur and certified management trainer Gary Johnson which provides resources for educators and thousands of pages containing information for math, geography, language, art and literature homework assignment. The address for Gary's Home Help Page website is *www.homeworkhelppage.com*.

National Cancer Institute—Dr. Andrew C. von Eschenbach serves as the organization's Director. Correspondence can be sent to Public Inquiries Office, National Cancer Institute, Suite 3036A, 6116 Executive Boulevard, MSC8322, Bethesda, MD 20892-8322. The organization can be contacted by telephone at 1-800-422-6237. Visit its website at *www.cancer.gov*.

National Diabetes Information Clearing House—1 Information Way, Bethesda, MD 20982-3560. Telephone: 1-800-860-8747 or 301-654-3327. Facsimile: 301-907-8906. Its website address is *www.diabetes.niddk.nih.gov* and its e-mail address is *ndic@info.mddk.nih.gov*.

National Fatherhood Initiative—101 Lake Forest Boulevard, Suite 360, Gaithersburg, MD 20877. For general information, Mondays through Fridays from 9:00 AM to 5:00 PM, call 1-800-790-DADS. Its office telephone number is 301-948-0599. Its facsimile number is 301-948-4325.

MASSACHUSETTS
Joslin Diabetes Center—One Joslin Place, Boston, MA 02215. Telephone: 617-732-2400. Its website address is *www.joslin.harvard.edu.* *www.joslin.harvard.edu*

Judge Baker Children's Center—Alvin F. Poussaint, M.D. serves as the Director of the organization's Media Center. Mailing address: 3 Blackfan Circle, Boston, MA 02115. Telephone: 1-800-779-8390—extension 2109. Facsimile: 617-232-8399. Visit its website at *www.jbcc.harvard.edu.* Its e-mail address is *info@jbcc.harvard.edu.*

MINNESOTA
National Coalition of Free Men—Post Office Box 582023, Minneapolis, MN 55458-2023. Visit the organization's website at ***www.ncfm.org.*** E-mail messages can be sent to *ncfm@ncfm.org.*

NEW JERSEY
African American Male Empowerment Summit[SM]—614 Central Avenue, Suite 3, East Orange, NJ 07018. Telephone: 973-414-8644. Facsimile: 973-414-8684. The website address is *www.aames.org* and its e-mail address is: *info@aames.org.*

NEW MEXICO
The National Hispanic/Latino Community Network—Post Office Box 2215, Espanola, NM 87532. Telephone: 505-747-1889. Facsimile: 505-747-1623.

NEW YORK
American Cancer Society—19 West 56th Street. Telephone: 212-586-8700. Facsimile: 212-237-3855. Visit the organization's website at www.cancer.org.

Education Center for Prostate Cancer Patients—380 North Broadway, Suite 304, Jericho, NY 11753. Telephone: 516-942-5000. Facsimile: 516-942-5025. Visit the organization's website address at *www.ecpcp.org.* E-mails can be sent to *info@ecpcp.org.*

OKLAHOMA
Tulsa Area Fathers Rights Association—The organization is headed up by Gregory Romeo. Visit the organization's website at *www.tulsafathers.org* and its online discussion group at *http://groups.yahoo.com/group/Tulsa_Area_Fathers-Rights_Association.* The organization can be reached by telephone at 918-447-3094; or by facsimile at 419-710-1976; or by e-mail at TulsaFathers@yahoo.com.

PENNSYLVANIA
BSI International, Inc.—Exclusive publisher and distributor of **IN SEARCH OF FATHERHOOD® FORUM FOR AND ABOUT THE FATHERS OF THE WORLD**, a quarterly international male parenting journal. Visit its website at *www.bsi-international.com* or its Fatherhood discussion group at *http://InSearchOfFatherhood®@msngroups.com.* Contact BSI International, Inc. at Post Office Box 3885, Philadelphia, PA 19146-0185. E-mail messages can be sent to bsi-international@earthlink.net.

Diabetes and Educational Research Center—Franklin Medical Building, 829 Spruce Street, Suite 800, Philadelphia, PA 19107. Telephone: 215-829-3426. Facsimile: 215-829-5807. Its website address is *www.diabeteseducationalandresearchcenter.org* and its e-mail address is *webmaster@diabeteseducationalandresearchcenter.org.*

National Center on Fathers and Families—Dr. Vivian Gadsden is the Executive Director of the National Center on Fathers and Families which is located at the University of Pennsylvania, 3440 Market Street, Suite 450, Philadelphia, PA 19104. The organization can be reached by telephone at 215-573-5500. Visit its website at *www.ncoff.gse.upenn.edu.*

Pure Quality Entertainment, LLC—Philadelphia-based parent company of Pure Quality Film Works, which is the producer and distributor of a documentary on African American Fathers. Another division, Pure Quality Publishing will publish two books on African American Fathers. Visit its website at *www.purequality.com.*

Single and Custodial Fathers' Network—Contact: John R. Sims, Jr., Executive Director of The Single and Custodial Fathers' Network at One Parks Bend, Suite 213, Box 31, Vandergrift, PA 15690. Telephone: 724-845-9767 or 724-388-3237.

TEXAS
Center for Successful Fathering, Inc.—13740 Research Boulevard, Austin, TX 78750. Telephone: 512-335-0761. Its web site address is *www.fathering.org.*

Faithful Fathering Initiative In Texas—Post Office Box 1702, Sugarland, TX 77487. Telephone: 281-491-DADS. E-mail messages can be sent to *peprw@worldnet.att.*

Fathers for Equal Rights, Inc.—1525 Elm Street, 1600 Pacific Building, Suite 870, Dallas, TX 75201. Telephone: 214-953-2233.

VIRGINIA
Diabetes Education Programs/American Diabetes Association—1701 North Beauregard Street, Alexandria, VA 22311. Telephone: 1-800-DIABETES; 1-800-342-2383. E-mail messages can be sent to *customerservice@diabetes.org.*

Great Dads—Contact Dr. Robert Hamrin, Founder and President of Great Dads at Post Office Box 7537, Fairfax Station, VA 22039. Telephone: 703-830-7500. Visit Great Dads' website at *www.greatdads.org*. E-mail messages can be sent to *grtdads@aol.com*.

WASHINGTON
The National Fathers Network—16120 N.E. Eighth Street, Bellevue, WA 98008-3937. Telephone: 425-747-4004—Extension 218. Facsimile: 425-747-1069. E-mail messages can be sent to the organization's Executive Director at *jmay@fathersnetwork.org*

WISCONSIN
Wisconsin Fathers for Children and Families—P.O. Box 1742, Madison, WI 53701. Telephone: 1-608-255-3237. Visit its website at *www.wisconsinfathers.org*. Its e-mail address is *wfcf@wi.rr.com*.

RECOMMENDED READING FOR FATHERS

365 Reflections On Fathers. Gabriel Cervantes and Dahlia Porter. Adams Media Corporation—1998.

A Father's Tear: Seeing The Grace Of God Through The Eyes Of Grief. Bob Stacy. College Press—1999.

Ashes To Ashes . . . Families To Dust. Dean Tong. Hampton Roads—1992.

Becoming A Father: How To Nurture And Enjoy Your Family. Paul Froelich and William Sears. LaLeche League International—1986.

Becoming Dad: Black Men And The Journey To Fatherhood. Leonard Pitts. Longstreet Press—1999.

Black Fatherhood: The Guide To Male Parenting. Earl Hutchinson and Alvin F. Poussaint, M.D. with illustrations by Albert Fennell. Middle Pas—1995.

Black Fathers: A Call For Healing. Kristin Clark Taylor. Doubleday—2003.

Don't Make Me Stop This Car! Adventures In Fatherhood. Al Roker. Simon & Schuster—2000.

Father And Child Reunion: How To Bring The Dads We Need To The Children We Love. Warren Farrell, Ph.D. Jeremy Tarcher/Putnam—A Division of Penguin Putnam, Inc.—2001.

Fathers' Rights: Hard-Hitting And Fair Advice For Every Father Involved In A Custody Dispute. Jeffrey Leving and Kenneth A. Dachman. Perseus Books—1998.

Fathers In Prison. Larry D. Wolfgang. Stone Creek Publications—1999.

FatherSongs: Testimonies By African American Sons And Daughters. Gloria Wade-Gayles. Beacon Press—1997.

Final Rounds: A Father, A Son, The Golf Journey Of A Lifetime. James Dodson. Bantam Books—1997.

How A Man Prepares His Daughters For Life. Michael Farris. Bethany House Publishers—1 1996.

Live-Away Dads: Staying A Part Of Your Children's Lives When They Aren't A Part Of Your Home. William C. Klatte. Viking Penguin—1999.

Multicultural Counseling With Teenage Fathers. Mark A. Kiselick. Sage Publications—August 1995.

Raising A Son: Parents And The Making Of A Healthy Man. Don Elium and Jean Elium. Ten Speed Press—1997.

Raising Black Children: Two Leading Psychiatrists Confront The Educational, Social and Emotional Problems Facing Black Children. James P. Comer, M.D. and Alvin F. Poussaint, M.D. Dutton Plume—October 1992.

Seven Secrets Of Successful Fathers. Ken R. Canfield, Ph.D. Tyndale Publishers—1993.

Swallowed By A Snake: The Gift Of The Masculine Side Of Healing. Thomas R. Golden, LCSW. Golden Healing Publishing LLC—2000 (Second Edition).

The Broken Cord: A Family's Struggle With Fetal Alcohol Syndrome. Michael Dorris. Harper Collins—1990.

The Good Son: Shaping The Moral Development Of Our Boys And Young Men. Michael Gurian. Jeremy P. Tarcher/Putnam—1999.

The Seven Habits Of Highly Effective Families: Building A Beautiful Family Culture In A Turbulent World. Stephen R. Covey, St. Martin Press—1998.

The Single Father: A Dad's Guide To Parenting Without A Partner. Armin A. Brott. Abbevile Press—1999.

The Ultimate Survival Guide For The Single Father. Thomas Hoerner. Harbinger Press—2002.

The Wonder Of Boys: What Parents, Mentors And Educators Can Do To Shape Boys Into Exceptional Men. Michael Gurian. G.P. Putnam's Sons—1996.

Uncommon Fathers: Reflections On Raising A Child With A Disability. Donald J. Meyer. Woodbine House—1995.

Why Men Are The Way They Are. Warren Farrell, Ph.D. Berkeley—1986.

Zen And The Art Of Fatherhood: Lessons From A Master Dad. Steven Lewis. Dutton Plume—1997.

PERMISSIONS

"The Politics of Fatherhood," authored by Stephen Baskerville, Ph.D., was initially presented as a paper at the Plenary Session of the Conference on The Politics of Fatherhood at Howard University in Washington, D.C. by Dr. Baskerville on 23 March 1999 and subsequently published on the website of *Fathering Magazine* at *www.fathermag.com.*

"Our Sons . . . Our Schools," authored by Warren Farrell, Ph.D. was initially published on the website of *www.dadsnow.org.*

"Santee, Columbine . . . Why Boys Are The Way They Are," authored by Warren Farrell, Ph.D. was initially published on the website of *www.dadsnow.org.*

"Letters To My Son" and *"My Son's Life"* were extracted from the first-in-a-series Fatherhood book project **IN SEARCH OF FATHERHOOD®** which was published by BSI International, Inc. in April 1998 and authored by the late L.T. Henry under the pseudonym of *"LT. The Drummer—Not The Football Player."* The aforementioned materials are published herein posthumously with the express permission of BSI International, Inc., the publisher of and exclusive owner of the rights to the **IN SEARCH OF FATHERHOOD®** book projects.

"A Funny Thing Happened To Me On My Way To Becoming A House Husband," authored by Dale J. Fraza was initially published on the website of *www.dadsnow.org.*

"Making A Box—My Father's Death," authored by Thomas R. Golden, LCSW was excerpted from his book *"Swallowed By A Snake: The Gift Of The Masculine Side Of Healing"* which is published by Golden Healing Publishing LLC.

"Maintaining Fatherhood Status," authored by Almas Jamil Sami' was initially published in the *Autumn (October) 2001* issue of **IN SEARCH OF FATHERHOOD® FORUM FOR AND ABOUT THE FATHERS OF THE WORLD** which is exclusively published and distributed by BSI International, Inc.

"The Labour Party And Fathers In The Netherlands—Negotiating Between The Wrinkles In The Lace Curtain," authored by Joep Zander was initially published in the *Winter (January) 2002* issue of **IN SEARCH OF FATHERHOOD® FORUM FOR AND ABOUT THE FATHERS OF THE WORLD** which is exclusively published and distributed by BSI International, Inc. The article also appears on Mr. Zander's website at *http://huizen.daxis.nl/zander/isof.htm.*